Encountering Christ

Homilies, Letters, and Addresses
of Cardinal Jorge Bergoglio

Scepter

Contents

CORPUS CHRISTI HOMILIES

HOMILIES AND ADDRESSES FOR PRIESTS

HOMILIES AND ADDRESSES FOR BISHOPS

ON THE SOCIAL DOCTRINE OF THE CHURCH

Crossing the Threshold of Faith: An Invitation

ঙ৩

Message for the Year of Faith

OCTOBER 1, 2012–FEAST OF ST. THÉRÈSE OF THE CHILD JESUS

Among the most striking experiences of the past few decades is the experience of encountering locked doors. Little by little, increasing insecurity has driven us to bolt our doors, hire protection services, install security cameras, and glance with mistrust at strangers who come to our door.

Nonetheless, there are still some villages where people leave their doors open. The closed door is really a symbol of our day. It is something more than a simple sociological fact; it is an existential reality that has imposed itself as a way of life. It has become a way of confronting reality, other people, and the future.

The bolted door of my house, the setting of my intimate life, my dreams, hopes, sufferings, and moments of happiness, is locked against others. And it is not simply a matter of my physical house; it is also my whole life, my heart. Fewer and fewer people may cross that threshold. The security of reinforced doors guards the insecurity of a life that is becoming more fragile, less open to the riches of life and love of others.

The image of an open door has always been a symbol of light, friendship, happiness, freedom, and trust. How we need to recover these things! The locked door does us harm, paralyzes us, and cuts us off from one another.

The Invitation of Faith

As the Year of Faith begins, paradoxically, the image that Pope Benedict XVI proposes is that of a door, one through which we must pass to be able to find what we need so badly. The Church, through the voice and heart of Benedict XVI, invites us to cross the threshold and take a self-determined, free step: to take heart and enter a new life.

The phrase "door of faith" takes us back to the Acts of the Apostles: "And when they arrived, they gathered the church together and declared all that God had done with them, and how he had opened a door of faith to the Gentiles" (Acts 14:27).

God always takes the initiative, and he does not want anyone excluded. God calls at the door of our hearts: "Behold, I stand at the door and knock; if any one hears my voice and opens the door, I will come in to him and eat with him, and he with me" (Rv 3:20). Faith is a grace, a gift of God. "Only through believing, then, does faith grow and become stronger...in a continuous crescendo, into the hands of a love that seems to grow constantly because it has its origin in God" (*Porta Fidei*, 7).

Entering through that door presupposes the beginning of a way or journey that lasts a lifetime. Today so many doors are open to us, many of them false ones, doors that invite us in a very appealing but deceptive way to go down some road, promising an empty, narcissistic happiness with an expiration date; doors that lead to crossroads where, no matter which path we choose, we will sooner or later face suffering and confusion; doors focused on the self, which wear out and offer no guarantee for the future. And while the doors of our homes are locked, the doors of the shopping malls are always open.

One passes through the door of faith, one crosses that threshold, when the Word of God is announced and the heart allows itself to be shaped by that transformative grace—a grace which has a concrete name: and that name is Jesus. Jesus is the door (see Jn 10:9). He, and only he, is and always will be the door. No one comes to the Father except through him (see Jn 14:6). If there is no Christ, there is no way to God. As the door, he opens the way to God, and as the Good Shepherd, he is the only one who looks after us at the cost of his own life.

Jesus is the door, and he knocks on our door so that we might allow him to cross the threshold of our lives. "Be not afraid... open wide the doors for Christ!" Bl. John Paul II told us at the beginning of his papacy. We must open the doors of our hearts like the disciples of Emmaus, asking him to stay with us so that we might pass through the doors of faith, allowing him to help us to understand the reasons we believe and then going out to announce them. Faith means that we decide to be with the Lord, to live with him, and share this life with our brothers and sisters.

We give thanks to God for this opportunity to realize the value of our lives as his children, through this journey of faith which began with the waters of our baptism, that unending and fruitful dew which makes us children of God and brothers and sisters in the Church.

The purpose of this Year of Faith is for us to encounter the God with whom we have already entered into communion and who wishes to restore us, purify us, raise us up, sanctify us, and give us the joy our hearts crave.

The Challenge of Faith

This Year of Faith is a call to deepen in our lives that faith we have already received. To profess our faith with our mouth implies living it in our hearts and showing it in our deeds; it is a public testimony, a public commitment. The disciple of Christ, a child of the Church, can never think that belief is a private matter. It is a significant and demanding daily challenge for everyone who is convinced that he who began the good work in us will continue to perfect it until the day of Jesus Christ (see Phil 1:6).

Looking at our own situation as missionary disciples we must ask ourselves what challenges crossing this threshold of faith has in store for us.

It challenges us to discover that the sad reality we see around us can change. Even though it seems that death reigns in its various forms, and that our history is governed by the law of the strongest (or the cleverest), and that hatred and ambition are the driving forces of so many human struggles, we are also absolutely convinced that it will ultimately change, because "if God is for us, who is against us?" (Rom 8:31).

It challenges us to have the heart of a child. It supposes that we won't be ashamed to still believe in the impossible. We can live in hope: the only thing that can give meaning to history and transform it. As God's children, we can ask unceasingly, pray without weakening, and adore him so that our vision may be transfigured.

It leads us to have "the same mind as Jesus Christ" (see Phil 2:5), so that each of us might discover a new way of thinking, communicating with and looking at one another, respecting one another, living family life, planning our futures, and living our vocations.

It means being active, trusting in the power of the Holy Spirit who is present in the Church and visible in the signs of the times. It means joining the constant movement of life, and of history, without falling into the paralyzing defeatism of believing that everything in the past was better. It is an urgency to think in new ways, offer new suggestions, and express a new creativity, kneading life with the new leaven of "sincerity and truth" (see 1 Cor 5:8).

It implies that we have eyes for wonder and a heart that is not a lazy creature of habit. We are able to realize that every time a woman gives birth, it is another bet placed on life and the future; that, when we guard the innocence of children we are guaranteeing the truth of tomorrow; that when we treat gently the life of a selfless elderly person, we are acting justly and embracing our own roots.

It means work lived with dignity. It means a vocation to serve with the self-denial of one who begins time and time again without giving in to weariness, as if it were all only one step on the journey towards the kingdom, the fullness of life. It is the quiet time of waiting after the daily planting; it is the contemplation of the gathered harvest, giving thanks to the Lord because he is good, asking him not to abandon the work of his hands (see Ps 138:8).

It demands that we struggle for liberty and life together with others. Even when the surrounding culture abandons its principles, we know with certainty that the Lord asks us to live justly, love goodness, and walk humbly with our God (see Mi 6:8).

It entails the ongoing conversion of our attitudes, the tone of our life. It demands a total reformulation, not just a patching up or a coat of varnish. It means accepting the new form that Jesus Christ imprints on whoever is touched by his hand and his Gospel of Life. It means doing something entirely new for society and the Church, because "He who is in Christ is a new creature" (2 Cor 5:17–21).

It leads us to forgive and to know how to bring out a smile. It means approaching every person who lives on the margins of existence and call him or her by name. It means caring for the fragility of the weakest and supporting their trembling knees in the certainty that whatever we do for the least of our brothers, we do for Jesus himself (see Mt 25:40).

It demands that we celebrate life. We let ourselves be transformed, for we have been made one with Jesus at the table of the Eucharist, celebrated in community. We go on from there, our hands and heart busy working on the great project of the kingdom, knowing that all the rest will be given us besides (see Mt 6:33).

It means being a Church of open doors. It's living in the spirit of the Vatican Council and of Aparecida,[1] not just to let people in, but to go out and fill the lives of the people of our times with the Good News.

It means being convinced of the Church's mission—to be a church that lives, prays, and works with a missionary outlook.

It is the acceptance of the newness of life in the risen Christ. We accept that he has been raised in our poor flesh to make it a sign of a new life.

Meditating on all these things, we look to Mary. May she, the Virgin Mother, accompany us as we cross the threshold of faith and bring the Holy Spirit over our Church, as in Nazareth, so that just like her we may adore the Lord and go out to announce the marvels he has done in us.

---

1. A meeting of the Latin American and Caribbean bishops in Aparecida, Brazil, May 13–31, 2007.

Accompanied by Mary, Standing by One Another

ↄↄ

Transcription of the Homily at the Mass for Life

BUENOS AIRES, MARCH 25, 2011–FEAST OF THE ANNUNCIATION

Someone once told me that today is the brightest day of the year, since it commemorates the day when God began to walk with us. God is received by Mary; her womb is transformed into an enclosed sanctuary by the Holy Spirit, covered by God's shadow, and from then on, Mary begins accompanying the life that has just been conceived: the life of Jesus. She awaits her child like any mother, with great eagerness, but even before his birth the difficulties begin. She takes on herself that life of difficulties. At the moment when she is nearly ready to give birth, she is required to set out on a journey to fulfill the civil law of the Romans—and she obeys it. Her baby boy is born without any comforts, and she stays right there with him. Jesus is practically born in the street . . . in a stable . . . in a corral. There is no place for him, and she remains at his side.

After her immense joy at receiving the shepherds and the magi, and the universal recognition of Jesus, comes the threat of death and the exile—and Mary accepts the exile. Later, she is there for the return, there for her boy's education and growth. She remains the companion of that growing life, with all its difficulties and persecutions. She remains beside the Cross, sharing

7

in his loneliness while they torture him unjustly all night. She is there at the foot of the Cross. She accompanies the life of her Son, and she accompanies his death. And in her profound loneliness she does not lose hope—and then she accompanies his resurrection filled with joy. Her work did not end there, however, because Jesus entrusted the newborn Church to her, and ever since she has walked beside it, standing by watchfully over its very life.

Mary the woman who received and accompanied Jesus' life to the end, accompanies us, too, with all the problems and joys that life bestows on us. The woman of silence, of patience, who puts up with pain and confronts difficulties, is also able to share deeply in the joys of her son. Mary, the woman who, in a time like our own, receives life and embraces it fully, does so to this day, for she continues to be there for us in the life of the Church.

Pope Benedict XVI wished to designate this year as the Year of Life. And on a day like today, when the life of God was inaugurated on earth, this Year of Life has as its beginning, its greatest weight, that life brought through Mary and accepted by her. And in this Year of Life, I believe it would be well to ask ourselves how we receive life, how we accompany it, because at times we don't realize how fragile life is. Perhaps we do not adequately take into account the dangers that a person has to go through, from conception until death. Do we know how to embrace life? The life of our children, both our own children and those who are not ours? Do we give these children incentives to growth? Do we know how to set boundaries as we raise them? And those children who are not ours, those who seem to be "no one's children"—are we concerned about them, too?

They are life; they are the breath of God! Or are we more concerned about taking care of our pets, that having no freedom from their instincts, return to us what we interpret as affection?

What is spent to care for a pet could provide food and education for a needy child. Do we care for the lives of children as they are growing up? Are we concerned about their companions? Are we concerned that they grow up mature and free? Are we concerned about their recreation, their entertainment? Life continues to grow, and Mary continues at our side. Do we remain steadfast, as Mary does? How about our parents and grandparents? Our in-laws? Are we there for them? Are we concerned about them? Do we visit them? At times, sad as it is, there is no choice but for them to be in a nursing home because of their state of health or family circumstances. But once they are there, do we spend a Saturday or a Sunday keeping them company? Do we care for that life that is coming to an end, that gave life to us?

In this Year of Life, the Pope wants us to see the whole course of life. At every step, Mary is there. The worst thing that can happen to us is to lack the love it takes to care for life. If there is no love, there is no room for life. Without love there is only egoism, and a twisted love of self. Today, we ask for Mary's love (and courage!) to help us care for life. We might ask: "But in a global civilization that feels so apocalyptic, how can we offer love in the midst of so many contradictions? How can we care for life all the way from beginning to end?" The great Pope Pius XI said something very bracing: "The worst things that happen to us are not the negative factors of civilization, but the lethargy of the good people."

Do you have the courage to set out on the path that Mary chose, caring for life from beginning to end? Or are you lethargic? And if you are, what is it that's putting you to sleep? Mary did not allow anesthesia to interfere with love! So today we ask her: "Mother, may we love seriously, may we not fall asleep, and let us not take refuge in the thousand and one varieties of anesthesia that this decadent civilization offers." Amen.

FOR CATECHISTS

The Task of a Catechist

၏

Letter to Catechists of the Archdiocese

BUENOS AIRES, AUGUST 21, 2010

"And when he entered Jerusalem, all the city was stirred, saying 'Who is this?' And the crowds said: 'This is the prophet Jesus from Nazareth of Galilee.'" —MATTHEW 21:10–11

The feast of St. Pius X and the celebration of the Day of the Catechist is a good opportunity to express my gratitude for our catechists' silent dedication and commitment to the ministry of catechesis.

Catechesis in Argentina is at a very special place in time because, as you know, the Third Catechetical Congress will be held in Morón in 2013. Their motto, "Anticipating the dawn, building hope," expresses so beautifully the words of the Concluding Document of the General Congress of Latin American Bishops in Aparecida:

> The Church is called to a deep and profound rethinking of its mission, and to relaunch it with fidelity and boldness in the new circumstances of Latin America and the world. It cannot retreat in response to those who see only confusion, dangers, and threats, or those who seek to cloak the variety and complexity of situations with a mantle of worn-out ideological slogans or irresponsible attacks. What is required is confirming, renewing, and revitalizing the newness of the Gospel rooted in

our history, out of a personal and community encounter with Jesus Christ that raises up disciples and missionaries (11).

In thanking our catechists, I ask the Lord wholeheartedly to rejuvenate them with his grace, since the renewal of pastoral catechesis will not depend "on grand programs and structures, but rather on new men and women who incarnate that tradition and newness, as disciples of Jesus Christ and missionaries of his Kingdom" (*Aparecida*, 11).

In our task of evangelization, God asks us to *accompany a people who walk in faith.* We always do well to remember that the child, youth, and adult whom God places on our path is neither a vessel to be filled with content, nor a person we must conquer. The Lord already dwells within their hearts; he always goes before us; he "precedes us."

The Faithful People We Serve

Our task is simply— and nothing less than—to help reveal and make known the presence of the One who is already present, who has all the power needed to fulfill every life. It's a beautiful mission, a ministry of the Word that catechists have performed continuously for nearly 2,000 years. It's a service to the Church that encompasses many different ways and places. For all this, I give you thanks and encouragement. Never cease to place yourself at the service of the holy, faithful people of God. Here are some qualities of these people whom you serve with such dedication.

They are a people in need of witnesses more than of teachers. I encourage you to unite catechesis with *kerygma*, so that the process and growth of faith have the freshness of the encounter with the One who strengthens you as a missionary disciple.

They are a people to whom you and I belong. Through baptism, we are a family, brothers and sisters in Jesus, healed of all our wounds as orphans.

They are a people whose life takes place in this beloved city. It's a city whose river we have often failed to protect but that gives us our identity as people of the port city of Buenos Aires, which is at once autonomous and dependent, much like Corinth in its lights and shadows.

They are a people whose faith is felt in their daily lives. They live in a city rich in its many shrines and familiar altars that, paradoxically, are more common in those neighborhoods that some regard as disposable or marginal.

They are a people in need of closeness—so that the anonymous majority may not kill even the smallest part of history, because the fact that it is human and Christian makes that little history sacred ground.

They are a people threatened more than ever by an increasingly pagan culture. That culture prides itself on its amnesia, intending to impose upon us a watered-down God, transcendent but within limits, always on hand to be used as an instrument of the consumerism that overwhelms us.

They are a people that need catechists more than ever. You ensure that the transmission of the faith in Buenos Aires can continue to be a cause for celebration and true encounter.

Catechists help make sure that the freshness of the child praying at night and the treasured wisdom of our elders may give our city real *buenos aires*—"good airs," winds of transcendence that come from heaven but make earth habitable. Without transcendence, we will be dominated by the inconsequential. It should come as no surprise, then, that with contaminated air, human nature also grows "biodegradable" within our city.

Precisely for these reasons, catechist, *your people and your city need you more than ever.*

Joyful, committed, renewed in your passion, continue to make ever present that style of the missionary Church that knows all about weaknesses—its own and those of others—and so reaches out, listening, embracing, accompanying.

Never get tired of sowing the seed! I encourage you to make a pilgrimage to the Parish of Our Lady of Mercy. And at the tomb of Mother Antula, through her intercession pray for yourself, pray for me, and pray for each of the catechists in this holy city who are *its greatness and its strength.* Plead to God for the grace to stand by our people and care for their faith, as Mother Antula was able to do three centuries ago, in difficult circumstances much like our present ones.

It will be a way of "anticipating the dawn, and building hope." May Jesus bless you and may the Blessed Virgin take care of you.

Embracing Life: Of Penalty Kicks and Mummies

Transcription of the Homily for the Archdiocesan
Catechist Encounter

BUENOS AIRES, MARCH 10, 2012

Today's theme is "With Mary's hands, let us embrace life." Let us nurture life so that it will grow; hold it close to protect it and receive it as Jesus did. One must not take a selective attitude toward life as it comes to us, unlike the scribes and Pharisees who murmured against Jesus: "This man receives sinners and eats with them" (Lk 15:2). Jesus received life as it was, not wrapped up in luxury packaging.

"This is life, and I receive it," Jesus would say. It's the same with soccer: You have to intercept penalty kicks wherever they come; you don't get to choose where anybody is going to kick them. Life comes at us like that; you have to receive it even if you don't like it.

That father in Luke 15 gave life to his sons, watched them grow, amassed a great fortune to leave to them. One day he is faced with a mere whim—a son gone astray—and he let this son take the lead in his own drama. He had already given advice, but it was ignored, so he disposes of his possessions in order to divide them between his sons. He knew this son would waste them, but that was the turn life took. He surely spoke with him and offered advice, but he let him do it. And the son left.

And the father, the Gospel says, saw him coming back in the distance. He saw him coming from afar because he would often go up to the roof, waiting and hoping for his return. He was waiting for his son—the shameless one, the thief, the one who had cost him dearly, the one who had morally been dragged through the mud. The role of the father was to await life as it would come—beaten, dirty, sinful, destroyed, however it would come. He had to await that life and then welcome it in a warm embrace.

Sometimes we defend ourselves by creating ultimatums like the scribes and Pharisees: "Until life is purified, I will not accept it." They used to wash their hands a thousand times before eating and praying. But Jesus reproaches them because their hearts were far from what God wanted—the God who sends his son to be one with the worst of us.

The friends of Jesus were the worst characters of all. But Jesus embraced life as it came. He allowed every man and every woman to play the role they wished in their own lives. He would accompany them lovingly, tenderly, with doctrine, with advice. He never forced anybody.

Life is not imposed. Life is planted and watered, but not imposed. Every person stars in his or her own drama. And God respects that. Let's embrace life the same way God does.

The father, who saw his son coming back home, was deeply moved. He was moved in spite of the human wreck that his son had become: an existential beggar who had shattered his soul and body, who was hungry. Deep inside he could have asked, "This bum who left with all the money, who wasted it, now he comes back because he's hungry? No! Let the butler deal with him; let him do penance, and later I'll see if I will meet with him." He could have acted that way, but no, the father does not treat life like that. Instead, he is deeply moved and runs to throw his arms around his lost son. And when the son wants to apologize, he simply covers his mouth with his embrace.

Let's live life with the heart of that father as we deal with others: "I don't know what you did, I don't know what you've done with your life, but I do know that you're my brother, and I must bring you Jesus' message."

The older son, however, takes the judgmental stance of the scribes and Pharisees: "I am pure, I've always been in the Church, I belong to Catholic Action, Caritas, I teach catechism. I thank you, Lord, because I am not like these other people, I'm not like this riffraff." And this son closes his heart and prefers to play the hypocritical purist rather than be moved by the tenderness that his father showed him. He does not know how to embrace life. Probably, the most this man can give is biological life—never life from the heart.

And then there was the party! Life and the encounter are a celebration. To embrace life means to allow ourselves to encounter one another as we are, as the other person comes, or as I find him. Life is always an encounter, one we must celebrate. Jesus has already told us: there will be much rejoicing for each one of these who come back home—an encounter.

I ask you, catechists, in your catechesis is there celebration, an encounter? Or is it simply finger-pointing at people with a stern "*No*," like an old teacher in times gone by? Is it *no*, or a celebration, a real encounter? Do you know what a party is, or are you a catechist-mummy, anchored only in formulating truths and precepts, but without tenderness or any capacity for an encounter?

I would like to see no apostolic mummies among you! Go to a museum where you'll fit in better. I want you to have hearts that are moved by life, no matter where it comes from, to know how to embrace life, how to speak of this life who is Jesus.

And so that you don't make the mistake of mummifying yourselves, remember "the hand of Mary," the mother of tenderness. Let us embrace life with the hands of Mary.

Projecting the Joy of Faith

Letter to Catechists of the Archdiocese
BUENOS AIRES, AUGUST 21, 2012

"In those days Mary arose and went with haste into the hill country, to a city of Judah. And she entered the house of Zechariah and greeted Elizabeth" —LUKE 1:39–40

It has become customary for me to write you a letter as we approach the feast of St. Pius X. Through it I want to greet each of you and thank you for your silent and faithful work each week, for the ability to make yourselves good Samaritans who offer a hospitality of faith by being familiar faces— brotherly hearts that transform, somehow, the anonymity of a big city.

This year, the Day of the Catechist brings us a great moment of grace that we've already begun to enjoy. Within two months we will begin celebrating the Year of Faith, which our Holy Father Pope Benedict XVI has called for in order to "rediscover the journey of faith so as to shed ever clearer light on the joy and renewed enthusiasm of the encounter with Christ" (Apostolic Letter *Porta Fidei*, 2).

It will certainly be a jubilee year. The Pope himself has extended to us an invitation to go through the "Door of Faith." Going through this door is a journey that lasts a lifetime, but we are all called to renew that process, particularly during this special time of grace. Therefore, this year I exhort you, as a pastor and a brother, to walk through this present time with the transforming power of this event.

We all remember the oft-repeated invitation of Bl. John Paul II: "Open wide the doors to the Redeemer." God calls us again: Open the doors to the Lord: the door of the heart, the doors of the mind, the doors of catechesis, of our communities . . . *all* the doors leading to the Faith.

A *Yes*, Personal and Free

When we open the door of faith, there is always a *yes*, which is personal and free. A *yes* that we give to God, who takes the initiative and approaches man in order to engage him in a dialogue where gift and mystery are always present.

It was a *yes* that the Virgin Mother was able to give in the fullness of time, in the humble village of Nazareth, so that then and there the weaving of the new and definitive covenant could begin, the one that God had prepared, in Jesus, for all of humanity.

It is always good for us to turn our gaze to the Blessed Virgin—even more so for those of us who, in one way or another, are entrusted with the task of accompanying our brothers and sisters, and, together with them, saying *yes* to the invitation to believe.

The Spirit Urges Us On

But catechesis would be seriously compromised if the experience of faith left us anchored and closed within our own private world, or within the structures and spaces that we have created over the years. To believe in the Lord always means going through the door of faith. It leads us to get out into the open, set off, and break free. . . . Never forget that the first Christian initiation in time and history culminated in a mission—it was a *visitation*. Luke clearly narrates the story: *Mary set off hastily, filled with the Spirit.*

The experience of faith places us in the experience of the Spirit, who urges us forward. There is nothing more opposed to the Spirit than settling down and closing oneself off. When we don't walk through the door of faith, that door closes, the Church turns inward, the heart closes in on itself, and fear and a bad spirit "spoil" the Good News. When the chrism of faith becomes dry and rancid, the evangelist no longer spreads his good fragrance but loses it, often becoming a cause of scandal and estrangement for many.

The Joy of Faith

The believer is meant to become the receptacle of the happiness seen through the entire Gospel, which resonates throughout all of history, now on the lips of Elizabeth: "Blessed is she who believed" (Lk 1:45), and again addressed to Thomas by Jesus himself: "Blessed are they who have not seen and yet believe" (Jn 20:29).

Today, more than ever, the act of believing must project joy. As in that joyful meeting between Mary and Elizabeth, the catechist must drench himself and his ministry with the joy of faith. Please allow me to share with you part of what the bishops of Argentina wrote earlier this year in a paper in which we outlined some common pastoral guidelines for the period 2012–2015:

> Joy is the doorway through which we announce the Good News and the consequence of living in faith. It is the expression that opens the way for the love of God, who is Father of all. We see this in the angel's announcement to Mary—the angel who, before telling her what is about to happen, invites her to

be filled with joy. It is also the message of Jesus, who invites us to trust and to meet God the Father: rejoice. This Christian joy is a gift from God that arises naturally from the personal encounter with the Risen Christ and our faith in him.

So I encourage you with the Apostle Paul: Rejoice, rejoice in the Lord always. May the catechesis with which you offer loving service be marked by that joy, the fruit of the nearness of the risen Lord ("the disciples were glad when they saw the Lord" [Jn 20:20]), which also reflects your kindness and your availability to follow God's call.

Never allow an evil spirit to spoil the work to which you have been summoned. An evil spirit has very concrete manifestations, which are easy to spot: anger, abuse, contempt, belittling, routine, backbiting, gossip.

The Nearness of Faith

The Virgin Mary during the visitation reveals another attitude we should imitate and embody: *nearness.* She literally set off in order to shorten the distance. She wasn't satisfied with hearing the news that her cousin Elizabeth was pregnant. She knew how to listen with the heart and therefore was moved by the mystery of life. Mary's closeness to her cousin implied an uprooting, not remaining focused on herself, but quite the opposite. The *yes* of Nazareth, inherent in every attitude of faith, became a *yes* matched by her action. She who became Mother of the Son by the Holy Spirit, moved by that same Spirit, became *a servant to all* because of love for her Son. A faith rooted in charity, capable of enduring discomfort in order to embody the teaching of God, who knows how to make his identity, his name, and his mission known as nearness: "and you shall call him Emmanuel."

The God of Jesus is revealed as a God who is a close friend of mankind. Jesus' style is distinguished by that pleasant proximity. We Christians learn that style in our personal encounter with the living Christ, an encounter that has to be the permanent commitment of every disciple. Overwhelmed with joy at that encounter, the disciple seeks to approach everyone to spread his joy. The mission is a relationship and therefore unfolds through proximity, creating personal ties sustained over time. The friend of Jesus makes himself close to everyone, reaches out to generate relationships that awaken and ignite an interest for the truth. Out of friendship with Jesus Christ comes a new relationship with others, who are always seen as brothers.[1]

Closeness is often a mark of catechetical gatherings of all ages (children, youth, adults). But distant professionalism can always creep in: the misconception of thinking ourselves to be the "teachers in the know," the exhaustion and fatigue that lower our defenses and harden our hearts. Recall that beautiful First Letter of Paul to the Thessalonians: "We were gentle among you like a nurse taking care of her children. So, being affectionately desirous of you, we were ready to share with you not only the gospel of God but also our own selves, because you had become very dear to us" (1 Thes 2:7–8).

A State of Mission

In addition, I ask you not to see the field of evangelization reduced to the catechumens. You are privileged to spread the joy and beauty of the faith to their families as well. Make yourselves the echo of the catechetical ministry of this Church of Buenos Aires, which wants to live in a *state of mission.*

---

1. CEA, Pastoral Guidelines for the Triennium 2012–2015

Look to the Virgin Mary, a thousand and one times. May she intercede so that her Son may inspire that timely word or gesture, enabling you to make catechesis the Good News for everyone, bearing in mind that the "Church grows, not by proselytism, but by attraction."

I am aware of the difficulties. We are at a very particular time in our history, even more so in this country specifically. The recent National Catechetical Congress held in Morón was very realistic in pointing out the difficulties of transmitting the faith in the midst of so many cultural changes. Perhaps on more than one occasion you may find fatigue overtaking you, uncertainty confusing you. You may even come to believe that it is impossible today to spread the faith, that it's good enough to simply transmit values.

The Certainty of Faith

For this very reason, Pope Benedict XVI invites us all to walk together through the door of faith and to renew our belief in the Church, and to believe that she can continue doing what she knows how to do, in the midst of light and shadow. It's a task that does not originate from a strategy aimed at mere conservation; rather, it is the root of a mandate from the Lord that gives us identity, belonging, and meaning. The mission stems from the certainty of faith—from that certainty which, in the form of the *kerygma*, the Church has been transmitting to men and women for over two thousand years.

It's a certainty that coexists with a thousand questions. Certainty of the faith is not ideology, moralism, or existential assurances, it is the living and nontransferable encounter with a person, with an event, with the living presence of Jesus of Nazareth.

The Enthusiasm of Faith

So I encourage you to live this ministry with passion, with *enthusiasm*.

> The word *enthusiasm* is rooted in the Greek *en theos*: "carrying a god within." This term indicates that when we are carried away by enthusiasm, a divine inspiration enters us and uses our person to manifest itself. Enthusiasm is the experience of an "active God within me" so that I may be guided by his wisdom and strength. It also implies the exaltation of the mood due to something that enkindles my interest; it implies joy and admiration caused by a powerful inner motivation. It is expressed as passion, zeal, courage, and commitment. It is opposed to discouragement, indifference, apathy, coldness, and disillusionment.
>
> The "active God within" us is the gift that Jesus gave us at Pentecost: the Holy Spirit. "And I will send you what my Father has promised. Remain in the city until you are clothed with power from on high" (Lk 24:49). And so what was announced by the prophets comes to be: "I will give you a new heart and put a new spirit within you: I will remove from your body the heart of stone and give you a heart of flesh. I will breathe my spirit in you" (Ez 36:26).[2]

We know perfectly well that this enthusiasm, this fervor the Lord calls us to have, cannot be the result of willpower or a simple change of mood. It is grace—an interior renewal, a profound transformation that is grounded in and supported by a Presence. He once called us to follow him, and now, once again, he comes within us to transform our fears into passion, our sorrows into joy, our enclosures into new visitations.

---

2. Ibid.

I ask the Lord to give you an open mind to recreate the dialogue and the encounter among those whom God has entrusted to you, and to give you a believing heart in order to keep shouting that he is alive and loves us as no one else does. There is a prayer card of Mary, Help of Christians that reads: "You who have believed, help me!" May she help us to remain faithful to God's call.

Do not forget to pray for me, that I, too, may be a good catechist. May Jesus bless you and may the Blessed Virgin take care of you.

CHRISTMAS EVE HOMILIES

Look for Him Where No One Else Would

ᴇᴼᴏ

Transcription of the Homily for Christmas Eve

BUENOS AIRES, DECEMBER 24, 2010

Reading this Gospel passage, we are struck by the precision with which St. Luke situates the time and place of the birth: the Emperor Augustus, a census, Quirinus, governor of Syria, everyone having to be enrolled in his city of origin. The moment when God bursts into history is marked exactly. He had done this earlier in another way, with callings such as Abraham's; with laws; with liberation, as in Egypt; through Moses or the prophets. He had broken in with his word; now he breaks in with his real Word—Jesus Christ, who is the Word of God. He bursts in, and he who had been accompanying us on our journey, for the first time plants himself right in the middle of our path. And what he had promised earlier through the prophets came true. He, the all-powerful, the Creator, the Transcendent, transformed himself into God with us. From now on this God would be close to us, not a God who must be sought in the orbit of the stars, but one at our side.

An Encounter with Jesus

That was the first time that Christ came and began to walk with us. He is going to come a second time, also historically, but we do not know the hour: only God knows it. He is going to come a second time, which will be decisive for each one of us, as he seeks us out and takes us to himself. That second time will be definitive for all of humanity, when, in his glory, he will transform the earth into his eternal paradise. He came a first time and is going to come a second, and between these two comings we find ourselves, because he comes a third time: He comes every year to remind us that he came and will come again.

The feast of Christmas is a resounding reminder of history and revelation of God who came to tell us that he is here, as it says so beautifully in the book of Revelation: He "stand[s] at the door and knocks" (Rv 3:20). He is at the door of your heart, calling on you. God is coming. Christmas reminds us that he came once, that he is going to come once more, and that he invites us to receive him every day. Christmas is the feast of the encounter, of meeting him for the first time, of the hope of meeting him both definitively and every day.

Christmas is an encounter with Jesus. On this holy night you are invited to ask yourself how you can meet Jesus, whether you are ready to meet Jesus, or whether you let yourself be carried along by life as if it were all just a game. No, Jesus is knocking at *your* heart; Jesus is telling you the same thing that the angel told the shepherds: a Redeemer has been born to *you*. He simply asks you to listen—or rather, he asks you to seek him. Today he invites us to seek.

And where should we look for him? The sign that was given to the shepherds is the same as always. I'll repeat it as it was told to them: seek him in a manger, in a stable. The sign is the same: *look for him where no one else would.* Don't look for him among the lights of the great cities; don't look for him in appearances. Don't look for him in all that pagan assemblage that is offered to us continually. Seek him in the unusual, in surprising places. Seek him like those shepherds who were told to look for a newborn child lying in a manger. Seek him there. Push away the foliage, and underneath you will find the shoots of life, in that simplicity, in that littleness.

Lower Yourself

In the grotto of Bethlehem today, in order to enter the place where Jesus was born, one has to crouch down, to lower oneself: to meet Jesus one has to make oneself small. Shed all pretension. Shed every ephemeral illusion; get down to the essential, to what promises you life, to what gives you dignity. Lower yourself: do not be afraid of humility. Today we are told that the higher you hold your head, the more important you are. The more vain you appear, the more power you have. The more one shouts and quarrels, the more discord one sows, the better. No, that's not the case! Lower yourself; make use of meekness. Listen and live together in peace. Recognize your dignity and that of others. Love and let yourself be loved.

This is the night of surprises. The night before last, something happened that moved me. At the Obelisk there were children, organized by the Archdiocese, making up a living crèche scene, and here on the other corner of the Obelisk was a Santa Claus who was greeting people and accepting letters. At one point he crossed over and said to the person directing the living crèche: "Let me sit here: I want to feel the Christmas spirit." He sat down, removed his mask and accepted reality. Don't let yourself be hidden by pride, nor vanity, nor by shouting or domineering. That will get you nowhere. Lower yourself, take a gamble on meekness, take a gamble on goodness. Look through the foliage of life, and there you will find what no one else understands, a child lying in a manger, wrapped in swaddling clothes. There you will find Jesus every day.

Do you know how to seek? Do you lower yourself to find him, or do you get dizzy from the thousand and one attractions of this pagan city? (Because this really is a pagan city.) There's no entry fee to meet Jesus. If you want to, simply enter. He needs your freedom: he needs you to accept the free gift of salvation. There is no other explanation for this mystery of the Nativity but the gratuitousness with which God comes to meet us.

Go forth and seek him! Or else look at her, the Mother—so simple and gentle—and ask her to take you by the hand to seek the child, who cannot be found in pride and vanity but only in the simplicity of all that is love, meekness, and goodness. Amen.

The Password

∂◎

Transcription of the Homily on Christmas Eve
BUENOS AIRES, DECEMBER 24, 2011

In his announcement to the shepherds, the angel gave them a sign by which they were to find the child: "And this will be a sign for you: you will find a babe wrapped in swaddling clothes and lying in a manger." The ordinariness, the simplicity, the self-evidence was itself to be the sign, and the whole narration of the Gospel passage has this rhythm of serenity, of simplicity, of peace, of meekness. What could be meeker than a newborn child resting there, in that cradle? It was very comfortable, with good hay, a nice mattress. There he was, calm and meek, and calling us to be the same.

This is what counts, and everyone who is called at all is called to this: to participate in the peace intoned in the Gospel's song, to participate in the unity, in the meekness. Later on, when this little boy had become a man and was preaching, he would say to the people: "Learn from me, for I am meek and humble of heart." It's a message that, after twenty centuries, continues to be relevant—against bad temper, arrogance, self-sufficiency, aggression, insult, tension, war, misleading information, defamation, and calumny. Meekness and unity—it is all one with what began here with this first sign. "This will be a sign to you." This is the "password" that he came to teach us.

Another striking point is that those who were called were somewhat marginalized. The shepherds were a rough gang in that period: one might almost say a mafia. Everyone was afraid of them; people would not entrust anything to them because of their bad reputation. They weren't those picturesque little shepherds in the movies with their little lambs—and yet they were invited to meekness, to unity.

Some intellectuals from the East, too, men of honesty and integrity, are invited and come from afar, from very far. They traveled until they finally arrived. This child, a little later, when he was preaching, would say: "Come to me, all who labor and are heavy laden, and I will give you rest." From early on in his preaching he would invite those who felt marginalized. But the great trap that is set for us by our self-sufficiency is to believe that we are something by ourselves—the trap of not sensing our own marginalization. If we do not feel ourselves marginalized from within, we are not invited.

This same child, later, when he was grown, would tell a story about those who believed in themselves and permitted themselves the luxury of rejecting a wedding invitation. They were ignored, and the banquet hall filled with men and women sought out and found at the crossroads.

This is the sign, the password, the signal: a newborn child lying in a manger who calls together all those who are marginalized. And no one can say that he himself is not marginalized. Open your heart, look within, and ask yourself: In what ways am I marginalized? How do I cut myself off from love, from peace, from mutual collaboration, from solidarity, from feeling myself to be a social being?

Jesus calls us to meekness, to peace, to solidarity, to harmony; for this reason this night is called the night of harmony, of peace, of love.

Close to the crib, then, do two things: first, feel yourself invited to the beauty of humility, of meekness, of simplicity; and second, seek within your heart the ways in which you are on the outside, marginalized, and let Jesus call you from your emptiness, your limitations, your egoism. Let yourself be caressed by God, and you will understand better what simplicity, meekness, and unity are.

LENTEN HOMILIES AND MESSAGES

To Fast Is to Love

cᔕᓚ

Lenten Message

ASH WEDNESDAY (FEBRUARY 25, 2009)

There are certain scenes that we end up getting used to just because we've seen them so often. The great risk of becoming accustomed to something is *indifference*: Now nothing surprises us, causes us to shudder, delights us, strikes us, or inspires us to question anything. This can happen with the sad sights that appear more every day in our streets. We become accustomed to seeing men and women of all ages begging or looking through the garbage, many old people sleeping on the corners or in the doorways of businesses, many boys in wintertime lying on the gratings of the subways where a little warmth arises. With habituation comes indifference: we are not interested in their lives, their stories, their needs, or their future. How often do their searching eyes make us lower our own in order to be able to continue on our way? Still, this is the landscape that surrounds us and we, whether we see it or not, are a part of it.

To this jaded heart comes a call that wakes it up and rescues it from the evil of indifference: "the trumpet that the prophet invites to sound," marking the beginning of Lent. And the Word of God, who loves all his children without measure, says to us tenderly, "Return to me with all your heart" (Jl 2:12). That is the desire of God: that we, who at times find ourselves living far from him, might return: not by force, not against our will, not out of fear, but with "our whole heart."

This is what is essential in this season we're beginning: accepting the invitation to enter more and more fully into the intimacy of God. It is a word of love for us, people who always tend to put the accent on "fulfillment." That's why that same God continues to tell us: "Rend your hearts, and not your garments" (Jl 2:13). Our deeds, our mortifications, our sacrifices only have value if they proceed from the heart, if they express our love.

One of the pillars of our Lenten preparation is fasting; but this should be based on love and lead us to a greater love. The fasting that God wants continues to be "sharing your bread with the hungry, and bring[ing] the homeless poor into your house; when you see the naked, to cover him" (Is 58:7), not turning your back on your brother.

These days, one can only fast by working so that others need not fast. Today one can only celebrate a fast by taking on oneself the suffering and powerlessness of millions of hungry people.

One who does not fast for the poor is cheating God. To fast is to love. Our voluntary fasting should help to prevent the obligatory fasts of the poor. Let us fast so that no one else is forced to.

This Ash Wednesday, the Church of Buenos Aires is once more beginning "The Lenten Gesture of Solidarity." We want it to be the response of a community of disciples who are preparing to follow a path of conversion in order to truly fast. It is a fast that is a sign of solidarity with those who are fasting involuntarily, a sign of justice in a cruel world where some people's stomachs are swollen from eating and others from not eating; a fast which is not an imposition but a need to show gratitude for the love dedicated to Jesus, who gave us—and still gives us—his life

Clear Your Heart of Weeds

c⁄ℐ∂

Lenten Message

ASH WEDNESDAY (FEBRUARY 14, 2010)

We are struck by the kindness with which the Church knocks at our heart today, with her motherly tenderness: Return to God; be reconciled with God. Do not harden your heart; listen to the voice of the Lord. Show yourself as you are in the presence of God: a sinner. Empty your heart; make room for our Lord to enter. The Church speaks to us like a mother and wants us to enter this time of Lent with the goal of traveling toward our Lord, going out to meet him. This meeting takes place in our heart. And so the Church provides this period—a time to cleanse our hearts of all those things that distract us from that meeting and interfere with it.

In the Gospel Jesus tells us that it's not a matter of applying makeup to the soul, but of changing it—with almsgiving and fasting, with attitudes of service and detachment, and with prayer. To make room in one's soul so that this meeting with our Lord will happen. But be careful—do not do this for appearance' sake, because the enemy of the Christian is hypocrisy. Jesus wants us to have an open heart. He cannot accept hypocritical attitudes. This is why he tells us to clear our heart of weeds. "But how, Lord?" And he responds, "With prayer, penance, and alms." Yes, digging up weeds is hard, but thus our heart prepares us for that meeting with our Lord.

Return to God; let yourself be reconciled with God. Do not harden your heart; listen to the voice of our Lord. Make a place in your heart by means of prayer, penance, and almsgiving so that our Lord will come to you. This is the invitation of the Church at the beginning of Lent, and she imposes ashes on us to remind us of the vanity of everything other than Jesus, our Lord.

Receive the ashes with a great desire of returning to your Lord, being converted, not hardening your heart. Listen to the voice of your Lord, and make room in your heart so that you can meet him.

Escaping the Clutches of Habit

⤳

Lenten Gesture of Solidarity

BUENOS AIRES, FEBRUARY 17, 2010

"Working together with him, then, we entreat you not to accept the grace of God in vain." —2 CORINTHIANS 6:1

One of the most debilitating things is to fall into the clutches of habit. This goes for good as well as bad habits. When husbands or wives get used to affection and family life, they fail to realize its value, to be thankful, and to care diligently for what they have. When we become used to the gift of faith, Christian life becomes routine and repetitive. It no longer gives life meaning; it stops acting as leaven. Routine is a brake, a hardening that imprisons the soul. We trudge along, and we lose the ability to smile, to really look at other people and respond to them.

We are in danger! As a society we have, little by little, become used to hearing and seeing distasteful news every day through the media. What's worse, we have also become accustomed to seeing it and feeling it around us without it calling forth any response, or at most, a superficial and noncommittal comment. The wound is in the street, in the neighborhood, in our homes, but like deaf and blind people, we live with the violence that kills, destroys families and neighborhoods, gives rise to wars and conflicts in so many places, and we look at it as just one more video. The suffering of so many peaceful and innocent people has ceased to shock us; disregard for the rights of persons and whole peoples, poverty and misery, the rule of corruption, the drug assassin, forced child prostitution: it all becomes commonplace, and we pay without asking for a receipt, although sooner or later we are going to get the bill.

All of these realities, and many more, are not silent. They cry out to each and every one of us and speak to us of our limitations, our weakness, our sin—in spite of the fact that *we have gotten used to it.*

Becoming used to something tells us seductively that there is no sense in trying to change it, that we cannot do anything in the face of it, that it's always been that way, and that, anyway, we'll survive it. We give up our opposition, allowing things "to be what they are"—or at least what some have decided they are.

Lent, providentially, comes to awaken us, to shake us out of our drowsiness, from our walk of inertia. The words of Joel are a clear invitation: *return to God.* Why? Because something is not right—in us, in society, or in the Church—and we need to change, to reverse direction, to be converted. Something new *is* possible, simply because our faithful God continues to be rich in goodness and mercy, always ready to forgive and begin again.

We are invited to undertake a Lenten path, a path which includes the Cross and renunciation. It is a path of real, not superficial, penance, a fasting of our heart. "Rend your hearts and not your garments" (Jl 2:13).

This is a path that challenges us to snap out of our habits. It challenges us to open our eyes and ears, but especially our hearts, all the way—to allow ourselves to be "disturbed" by what is happening around us. When we look deeply, beyond prefabricated answers, the life of our brothers, with their anxieties and hopes, will shake us out of our routine and put us in a different place— one that is not immune to danger. But only in this way, when someone's suffering wounds us, and the feeling of powerlessness grows deep enough to cause us pain, do we find our real path toward Easter. "For our sake he made him to be sin who knew no sin, so that in him we might become the righteousness of God" (2 Cor 5:21).

The "Lenten Gesture of Solidarity" that we have been carrying out in the Archdiocese for several years should be seen as a sign of something that ought to be our vital attitude of discipleship throughout the whole year. It's training our hearts so that we do not mutilate our capacity for surprise and sorrow, so that we are not indifferent to reality and can experience with concrete deeds that "we have not received the grace of God in vain."

Let us ask our Lady to place herself in our hearts, pointing out so many sorrows and urging us on to prayer, to penance, to alms, to doing without something that we like for the sake of Jesus in others. And let us pray for one another so that the exercise of loving our neighbor might make us grow in love for God, whom we seek from our heart, whom we adore, and with whom we want to find ourselves.

"Be Reconciled to God": An Eagle Among Turkeys

e<ô⊚

Transcription of a Homily for Ash Wednesday

BUENOS AIRES, MARCH 9, 2011

The practice of Lent begins with the rite of imposition of ashes, reminding us of what we are—earth and clay—and what we are going to be—ashes. But it would be very sad to think that that is all. We were earth taken up by loving hands, by a God who breathed on us and gave us life. In breathing on us, he placed his hope in us. God does have hope for us. We will be ashes, but ashes that bear the imprint of the love we have given on earth. Lent, in this context, speaks to us of the love with which we were created and the love we must carry with us and leave in the end.

Penance, prayer, and fasting: The stripping-down that we do during Lent is not masochism; rather, it is a smoothing out of the heart, the heart that selfishness was causing to shrivel up. This is why the Church says to us each year: "Look further, look to the horizon! God didn't make you to go around with a shriveled heart. God didn't make you for egoism, or for yourself alone—he made you for love." This is why St. Paul began that very beautiful sermon, which is like the watchword of Lent, saying: "We beseech you on behalf of Christ, be reconciled to God" (2 Cor 5:20). This is the cry of Lent: Let yourself be reconciled to God!

You may not feel that you are at odds with God. No, but your heart is shriveled because, just like the hypocrites in the Gospel, perhaps you are looking at yourself too much, focused on your comforts, your own affairs, your own belongings. Eventually God is set aside. Be reconciled with God! There is also that beautiful call of the prophet Joel who says to his people: "Return to me with all your heart, and rend your hearts and not your garments. Return to the Lord, your God." It is Jesus who reconciles us. Let us make room for Jesus so that he can reconcile us, and we will return to God with all our heart. We can do this through actions that are a little more emphatic than usual, that get rid of our egoism and expand our hearts, so that our horizons can open up. Lent is not a time to be sad, with long faces (as Jesus says in the Gospel); it is for gazing out at that horizon of love and opening our hearts, letting those desires for something great rise up within us.

Some time ago I read a parable written by a monk which enlightened me greatly about this shriveling of the heart and how, at times, the world tends to press us in upon ourselves. The parable goes like this: Some boys climbing a mountain found an eagle's nest with an egg, and they brought it down with them. Later they wondered what they should do with the egg, and one of the boys suggested that they take it to his house, since he had a turkey hen that was sitting on some eggs to be hatched. So they added the egg to the ones the turkey was sitting on. The chicks were hatched, they all looked the same, and they started growing. But the eagle chick acted differently from the rest. When the others walked along looking at the ground, he looked at the sky and felt something. But since he had no one to teach him to fly, his life, which ought to have been spent flying high, was spent in the coop among the turkeys.

Together with this call to "be reconciled with God" and to "turn to God with all your heart," we can also ask ourselves this question: Am I in the turkey coop, or do I feel a desire to fly? Am I attached to a flock which is going along blindly doing what everyone else does, seeking only its own satisfaction, concentrating on self, or am I looking upward to fly high? I assure you that if, during this Lent, you look higher, pray more, and fast from things which entertain you in a negative way and instead take advantage of that time to do a good work: visiting a sick person, keeping your children company, listening to your father, or your grandfather, who says the same thing over and over— if you do this during this Lent, your heart will begin looking up and you will find a great surprise at the end.

May your shriveled heart, which is now practically a tomb, begin to feel that this tomb is the witness of someone who rose to save you, and you will encounter the living Jesus. So we begin Lent with a healthy optimism, with this great hope: Reconcile yourself with God; return to the Lord with your whole heart; let your heart grow larger; look upward! He will do the rest. Have confidence.

The Fasting that God Wants

e⁀⊙

Lenten Gesture of Solidarity

BUENOS AIRES, MARCH 9, 2011

The criteria of immediacy and efficiency have little by little invaded our culture. We want the maximum return with the least exertion. We sacrifice effort, time, profound values, and even vital concerns for short-term objectives that present themselves as socially or economically satisfying. The Christian life of faith is not immune to this philosophy, which is almost universally accepted. Although the faith of a disciple is strengthened and grows through the encounter with the living Jesus, reaching into all corners of life, and nourished by the experience of looking to the Gospel in order to live it as the Good News that illuminates our daily path, we run the risk of glancing at it "sideways" and seeing it only partially.

After proclaiming the Sermon on the Mount, Jesus said, ". . . that they may see your good works and give glory to your Father who is in heaven" (Mt 5:16). In the face of such a clear statement, can we be satisfied with doing a few good works? What our Lord proposes is more ambitious. He is calling for a work "out of goodness," which has its root in the power of the Spirit, poured out dynamically as a gift of love throughout our whole life. It's not just a matter of doing good deeds, but of acting with goodness. We are on the threshold of Lent, and one

temptation we might face is that of reducing it to a few particular good practices which end at Easter, wasting the flow of grace
that this time of conversion could have meant for our whole life.

Our True Fast

Our Lenten fast can be routine, becoming more a Manichaean than
a prophetic gesture, amounting to "closing the mouth" because
matter and food are impure. But the fasting that God wants is for
us to share our own bread with the hungry; to deprive ourselves not
only of what is superfluous, but even what is necessary in order to
help those who have less; to give work to those who have none; to
heal those sick in body or in spirit; to take care of those who suffer the scourge of drugs; to help to prevent the fall of so many; to
denounce all injustice; to work so that so many suffering people,
especially children on the street, cease to be common scenery; to
give love to the lonely, and not only when they come to us.

Do not think that it is eating or not eating that matters.
What makes the fast true is the spirit with which one eats or
fasts. If suffering hunger were a blessing, all the world's hungry
would be blessed, and we would not have to concern ourselves.
"No act of virtue can be great if it is not also of help to others. . . . Thus, no matter how much one spends the day in
fasting, no matter how much one sleeps on the hard ground, and
eats ashes, and sighs continually, if one does not do good to others, one is not doing anything great" (St. John Chrysostom).

Jesus fasted according to the tradition of his people, but he
also shared the tables of the rich and the poor, the just and sinners (see Mt 11:19). Let us fast with concrete solidarity as a visible
manifestation of the charity of Christ in our life. Thus our fast will
have meaning as a prophetic gesture and efficacious action—we
fast so that others do not have to fast. To fast is to love.

We have to experience the profundity of not placing so much importance on the food with which we deprive ourselves as on the food that we make available to a hungry person through our privations. May our voluntary fast be what prevents so many involuntary fasts among the poor. Let us choose to fast so that no one else is forced to.

Now that Lent has begun, blessed are those forty days if we train our hearts to a permanent attitude of sharing and re-sharing our bread, and our life, with those most in need. Our fast cannot be an occasional free gift but must rather be an invitation to grow in a freedom through which we see that he is not happiest who has the most, but who shares the most—because he has entered into the dynamism of God's gratuitous love.

We live in a time marked by mission, not as an extraordinary gesture but as a way of being the Church in Buenos Aires. We want each pastoral gesture to be not an end in itself but the mark of a beginning, generating a lasting attitude. With this in mind, we hope our "Lenten Gesture of Solidarity," will allow us to bear witness to the Good News, so that, through our baptism, we may be a family which feels as their own the anguish and sufferings of everyone, every day of the year.

I would like to thank you for all you have accomplished through this "Gesture" in previous years, and I encourage you to let your living charity be the sign that authenticates our proclamation of the kingdom.

May God bless you and grant you a holy Lent lived in the love of God for his people.

Freely You Have Received, Freely Give

Lenten Message
ASH WEDNESDAY, FEBRUARY 22, 2012

One of the greatest dangers lying in wait for us is "getting used to it." We become so used to life and to everything in it that nothing surprises us—neither the good, to give thanks, nor the evil, to truly sadden us. I am surprised and perplexed when I ask an acquaintance how he is, and he replies: "Bad, but I'm used to it."

We get used to getting up each day as if there were no other way of seeing things. We get used to violence as something that's unavoidable. We get used to poverty and misery habitually walking through the streets of our city. We get used to seeing women and children at night in the inner city carrying away the castoffs of others. We get used to living in a paganized city where children do not know how to pray or make the Sign of the Cross.

Getting used to things anesthetizes the heart, destroying the capacity for that amazement that renews us in hope. We are left with no room for the recognition of evil and the power to struggle against it.

On the other hand, there are moments so powerful that they shock us out of this unhealthy perspective and reveal a reality that challenges us a little more each time. For example, when we lose some very beloved person or thing, we tend to value and be thankful for what we have—what, a moment earlier, we hadn't

51

really appreciated. Along our journey as disciples, Lent presents that powerful moment, that turning point that brings our hearts out of the routine and laziness of habit.

Thanksgiving and Conversion

Lent, in order to be authentic and fruitful, far from being a mere time of observance, is a time of conversion, of returning to the roots of our life in God. It's a conversion that blossoms from thanksgiving for all that God has given us, for all that he has accomplished and continues to accomplish in the world, in history, and in our personal lives. It's a thanksgiving like that of Mary, who, in spite of the troubles she had to endure, did not adopt a defeatist outlook but instead sang of the greatness of God.

Thanksgiving and conversion go together. "Repent, for the kingdom of heaven is at hand," proclaimed Jesus at the beginning of his public life. Only the beauty and gratitude of the kingdom win the heart and move it to real transformation—thanksgiving and conversion, known to all who received freely from the hands of Jesus health, forgiveness, and life.

Jesus, when sending his disciples out to announce that kingdom, told them: "Give freely." The Lord wants his kingdom to be spread through acts of gratuitous love. Thus, men recognized the early Christians as bearers of a message that overflowed from them. "Freely you have received, freely give." I would like these words of the Gospel to be engraved very deeply on our Lenten heart. The Church grows by attraction, by witness—not by proselytism.

Love Generously

Our Christian conversion has to be a grateful response to the marvelous mystery of the love of God that he worked though the death and resurrection of his Son, which becomes present to us in every birth to the life of faith, in every act of forgiveness which renews and heals us, in every Eucharist which sows in us the very feelings of Christ.

In Lent, by conversion, we turn to the roots of the faith by contemplating the immeasurable gift of the Redemption, and we realize that everything has been given to us by the free initiative of our God. Faith is a gift of God that cannot fail to lead us to thanksgiving and then to passing on its fruit in love.

Love shares everything it has: it reveals itself through being communicated. There is no true faith that is not manifested in love, and love is not Christian if it is not generous and concrete. A decidedly generous love is a sign of and invitation to faith. When we care for the needs of our brethren, like the Good Samaritan, we are announcing and making present the kingdom.

Thanksgiving, conversion, faith, generous love, and mission: these are key words for praying at this time, as well as embodying them through the "Lenten Gesture of Solidarity" which has so edified our church of Buenos Aires during these last few years. I wish you a holy Lent. May Jesus bless you, and the Blessed Virgin watch over you. And, please, I ask you to pray for me.

"I Will Arise and Go to My Father"

∞

Transcription of the Homily for Ash Wednesday

BUENOS AIRES, FEBRUARY 13, 2013

The Church's gaze on this first day of Lent is directed at our heart and its relationship with God, as we see in the first prayer: "We are beginning a path of conversion." What God wants is a converted heart. He longs for us to take one more step on that path towards him, our Father, who is all tenderness, mercy, and forgiveness. Therefore, before the Gospel, the celebrant repeats the phrase, "Today, when you hear his voice, harden not your hearts" (Heb 3:7–8). Listen to the voice of God so that your heart is freed from the calluses of sin, the hardness of being deaf to the things of God, the self-sufficiency that lets everything slide off. For this reason we are invited to repent, to be converted.

To convert is to be at peace with God, to be reconciled with God. Paul told the Corinthians, "We beg you in the name of Christ, please, allow yourself to be reconciled to God." But how? None of us, by our own strength, are able to be reconciled with God. It is Christ who came to do this. Paul himself says it: Christ is in the world, reconciling the world to God. That's his job! He is the peacemaker, the one who came to restore us to harmony with God.

Allow yourself to be reconciled—this is what the Church tells us today. Let Jesus work in your heart to reconcile you with

54

the Father. To live reconciled to God is to live in peace with him; to live reconciled to God is to savor his paternal tenderness; to live reconciled to God is to allow yourself to enjoy the banquet that was held for the son who had left his father's house and squandered his goods, the son who one day felt grace in his heart and said: "I will arise and go to my father."

That's the phrase that now, perhaps, we can each say: "I will arise, in whatever way I can, and go to my father." Each year we will find something that allows us to be reconciled with God. So this year let us do what little we can. Once you've make that decision, through Jesus who alone reconciles—then comes the celebration, the new beginning, the beginnings of a new heart, and that is what I wish for all of you, and for myself, too. May this first day of Lent encourage us to begin with a new heart. May Jesus continue renewing us, and let us say: "I will arise and go to my father; I will launch into life with my new heart." Amen

Escaping the Trap of Powerlessness

⟶⟵

Lenten Message

BUENOS AIRES, FEBRUARY 13, 2013

"Rend your hearts, not your garments, and return to the Lord, your God, for he is gracious and merciful, slow to anger, and abounding in steadfast love."—JOEL 2:13

Little by little, we have grown accustomed to hearing and seeing the dark chronicle of contemporary society, presented in the media with a sort of perverse enjoyment. We are also accustomed to touching and feeling it around us. The drama is in the streets, in the neighborhood, in our homes, and—why not?—in our hearts. We live with violence that kills, destroys families, and causes wars and conflicts in so many countries of the world. We live with envy, hatred, calumny, and worldliness in our own hearts. The suffering of innocent and peaceful people never ceases to beat against us; contempt for the rights of individuals and the most fragile peoples are not so foreign to us, either. The rule of money with its devilish effects, such as drugs, corruption, trafficking in human beings—even children—together with material and moral misery: These are common currency. The destruction of dignified work, painful emigrations, and the lack of a future are also added to this symphony. Our errors and sins as the Church are not lacking in this great panorama. The most private acts of selfishness are justified, but not therefore diminished. The lack of ethical values within a society metastasizes in its families, in the life of its neighborhoods, villages, and cities; they speak to us of our limitations, our weakness, and our incapacity to transform this endless list of destructive realities.

The trap of powerlessness leads us to think: *Is there any point in trying to change all of this? Can we make any progress in the face of this situation? Why bother, when the world continues its carnival dance, concealing it all under a disguise?* Nevertheless, when the masks fall off, the truth will appear and, although for many it sounds anachronistic to say so, sin will appear again, wounding our flesh with all its destructive force, twisting the fate of the world and of history.

Lent presents itself to us as a cry of truth and sure hope. It comes to tell us that it is possible not to put on a plastic smile as if nothing were wrong. It is possible for everything to be new and different, because God continues to be "rich in goodness and mercy, always ready to forgive," and he encourages us to begin again and again. Today we are invited once more to undertake an Easter pathway towards life, one that includes renunciation and the Cross, one that will be uncomfortable but not fruitless. We are invited to recognize that something has gone wrong in ourselves, in society, and in the Church—to change, to make an about-face, to be converted.

Today, the words of the prophet Joel are strong and challenging: "Rend your hearts and not your garments: return to the Lord your God." They are an invitation to all peoples—no one is excluded.

Rend your hearts—not your garments by an artificial penance without promises for the future.

Rend your hearts—not your garments by a formal, "technical" observance of the fast, which leaves us well filled.

Rend your hearts—not your garments with a superficial and selfish prayer which fails to reach the depths of our own life to allow it to be touched by God.

Rend your hearts and say with the Psalmist: "We have sinned." As St. Gregory the Great said, "The wound of the soul is sin: O poor wounded one, recognize your physician! Show him the wounds of your guilt. And given that our secret thoughts are not hidden from him, make him hear the groan of your heart. Move him to compassion with your tears, with your insistence. Importune him! May he hear your sighs, make your pain reach him so that, in the end, he can say to you: The Lord has forgiven your sin." This is the reality of our human condition. This is the truth that can bring us to real reconciliation with God and with man. It is not a matter of disparaging our self-esteem, but of penetrating to the depths of our heart and making us aware of the mystery of suffering and sorrow that has bound us for centuries, for millennia, forever.

Rend your hearts so that through this opening we will truly be able to see ourselves.

Rend your hearts, because only into broken and open hearts can the merciful love of the Father who loves us and heals us enter.

Rend your hearts, says the prophet, and Paul begs us, almost on his knees, to "be reconciled with God." To change one's way of life is a sign and fruit of a heart that is rent and reconciled by a love that is beyond us.

This is the invitation, in the face of so many wounds that harm us and harden us. *Rend your hearts*—experience in silent and calm prayer how sweet is the tenderness of God.

Rend your hearts, in order to feel the echo of so many torn lives, lest indifference leave us inert.

Rend your hearts, in order to love with the love with which we are loved, to console with the consolation which consoles us, to share what we have received.

The liturgical season that the Church begins today is not only for us, but also for the transformation of our families, our community, our Church, our native land—the transformation of the whole world. They are forty days in which to be converted to the very holiness of God. We become collaborators who receive grace and the chance to build up human life so that every man can experience the salvation that Christ gained for us through his death and resurrection.

Together with prayer and penance, as a sign of our faith in Easter's power to transform everything, we also prepare ourselves, as we do every year, to begin our "Lenten Gesture of Solidarity." As the Church of Buenos Aires, setting out toward Easter and believing that the kingdom of God is possible, we need to let the flow of grace spring from our hearts, torn open by love and the desire for conversion and the effective gesture that relieves the pain of so many of our brethren. "No act of virtue can be great if it is not followed by advantage for others . . . So, no matter how much you fast, no matter how much you sleep on a hard floor and eat ashes and sigh continually, if you do no good to others, you do nothing great" (St. John Chrysostom).

This Year of Faith that we are living is also an opportunity that God is granting us to grow and mature in that encounter with our Lord who becomes visible in the suffering faces of children without a future, in the trembling hands of the forgotten elderly, and in the unsteady knees of so many families who continue to face life without finding anyone to support them.

I wish you a holy Lent, a penitential and fruitful Lent, and please, I ask that you pray for me. May Jesus bless you, and the Blessed Virgin watch over you.

EASTER VIGIL HOMILIES

Removing the Stone

e∕6∂

Transcription of the Homily at the Easter Vigil
BUENOS AIRES, APRIL 11, 2009

The women, who loved Jesus so much, got up very early to go and anoint his dead body. They were convinced: he was dead. It was over. A beautiful illusion was over. It was time to face life and go on as well as they could. But love had brought them to this, and here they were, concerned about who would open the tomb for them: a rounded stone, turned to seal the entrance to the sepulcher. It was a very large stone. This worried them. They discussed it. "Who will roll away the stone for us?" (Mk 16:3). The rest we know: They found the stone removed, the angel announced that Jesus was alive, and then they ran away, trembling, saying nothing to anyone because they were dying of fright.

As I was listening to the Gospel, I thought of the centuries we have relived here today, with the reading of the history of salvation, the Jewish people, the People of God—all those centuries of history are dashed and collapse before a stone that it seems that no one can move. All the promises of the prophets, the enthusiasms and hopes, end here, dashed on a stone. And I thought of the history of our lives. We all have our history, with pros and cons, good and bad. Not centuries, but years and years of histories. And we all have our faith in Jesus.

And then I wonder: How often is our Christian life nothing more than going along and worrying about who is going to move a stone for us? And this is how we pass through life! Will this work out, or won't it? How can we manage this matter or that other one? Always facing a stone—which we realize that we can't move! And this ties us down, takes away our freedom, and keeps us from flying! It doesn't allow us to be ourselves. How many times, hours, days, weeks, months, and years are spent wondering who is going to move the stone for us? This is a fiasco.

When someone says to us: "Look, the stone has been moved; look, the one you were looking for is alive, at your side," we are seized by fear and take off like a shot! We prefer the safety of wondering who is going to move the stone to the danger of having him alive at our side! May we instead be inspired at each moment by something new, daring, and creative! All this is inspired in us by the life of the Risen One.

Today, looking at these women, let us ask ourselves about our own lives. Let us ask ourselves if we are convinced that the stone has been moved away and there is no one inside. And if you are truly convinced, why are you wasting time worrying about who is going to remove the difficulty for you? You have him living at your side—the Risen One! He is alive! He is with us! Instead of feeling the sadness of worrying about who is going to move the stone of difficulty, you will feel the wonder of the encounter with him, and it will transform your life!

Tonight let us say to Jesus: "Lord, may I feel the wonder of meeting you. Let me not entangle my life in questions about whether this or that will happen, or if I will or won't be able to do something. Instead, may I feel the happiness, the wonder, the joy, and the amazement of knowing you are risen, living at my side, and may I know that this is not a piece of fiction."

Two paths remain for us: We either believe in the stone that seals the tomb, wondering who is going to move it, or we believe that he has already left the tomb and accompanies us. What we are celebrating today is the latter: He is alive. May we let ourselves meet him so that our lives might be transformed. Amen.

Walking in Hope

ఆ@

Transcription of the Homily at the Easter Vigil
BUENOS AIRES, APRIL 3, 2010

As we read in the Gospel of St. Luke about the women at the open tomb, we see a number of feelings expressed on that Sunday morning: The women are confused because they see the tomb open; they are filled with fear, not daring to raise their eyes from the ground. When they return from the tomb, they tell what happened to the eleven, who think they are delirious and don't believe them. Peter goes, and he returns full of amazement. There's a mixture of bewilderment, fear, delirium, amazement. . . . They seem to be caught in a situation that they don't understand and can't interpret, a meaning they can't grasp—and, then, for good measure, an angel says to them: "Why do you seek the living among the dead?" (Lk 24:5) And the angel has to explain to them: "Remember how he told you, while he was still in Galilee, that the Son of Man must be delivered into the hands of sinful men, and be crucified, and on the third day rise?" (vs. 6–7). The women then remembered his words.

These women and the disciples were imprisoned because they had "forgotten." They had "forgotten" the Lord's words, and they needed an angel to shake them up and tell them to recall what he'd promised and have hope. They were the first Christians without hope to appear in history. They lost hope in their Lord because they had forgotten his prophecy, they had forgotten his prom

65

ise—they were ensnared in the dynamic of the moment. It is so easy to fall into this trap, to be a Christian without hope. You are a Christian; you go to Mass on Sundays, but do you really believe that Jesus is alive within you? In the midst of your family? In all areas of your life? Do you walk with the living Lord?

All too often we act as if our Lord was buried, with the stone at the entrance of the tomb well fixed. We are not going to get anywhere this way. If we don't remember the prophecy, if we don't hold onto what Jesus himself told us, we will have no hope. We will be a prisoner of the moment—the surprise, convenience, fear, and unbelief of the moment. St. Peter told the early Christians that they should be prepared to give a reason for their hope, that they should have the courage to say, "I walk like this because I hope! I walk and act like this because I know the Lord will come. I want him to find me watching, on guard, and with hope that is founded on the memory of Jesus' promise: 'I am going to rise and I will be with you all days, until the end of the world'" (Mt 28:20). Do we believe this?

I want this Easter to revive our memory about what Jesus said about himself. In that memory our hope will be rooted, and we will walk in hope—which is not the same as walking in optimism, by the way. Optimism is a psychological attitude, while hope is a gift of God, a virtue that God puts in your heart that is rooted in his promise not to let you lose your way. This is the hope of that anchor that is thrown to the shore in the fullness of time, and we hold onto the rope of this anchor so that we don't lose our way in the midst of the various hopeless, pessimistic, or simply neutral proposals that life places in our heart—which, in the end, do not satisfy us but leave us sad, as those who are just drifting along.

Grasping this cable of hope, remembering what Jesus promised us, let us go forward, recalling what the angel has told us: "Do not seek the living among the dead." Amen.

Beyond a Tomb, There Is Always Hope

ᴄᴓ

Homily at the Easter Vigil
BUENOS AIRES, APRIL 23, 2011

Sunday was dawning when the women who loved Jesus so much went to visit the tomb—the tomb blocked by the stone that Joseph of Arimathea had rolled there, which the uneasiness of his bad conscience led him to command that it be sealed and guarded (Mt 27:66). That stone conclusively sealed off the expectations of salvation that the life and preaching of Jesus had created. That stone, secured, sealed, and guarded by soldiers constituted a "refutation" of so many promises. That stone proclaimed a resounding failure, and those weakened women walked sadly toward that monument to the failure.

And then God said, *Enough!* Next came the earthquake and the angel of the Lord with the lightning-like power of a new truth that made the stone roll backwards; and the now-empty tomb was opened. And the angel said to the women: "He is not here; for he has risen, as he said" (Mt 28:6). And then they remembered that little ember of hope for which they had left no room in their hearts. Henceforth the followers of Jesus know that beyond a tomb there is always hope. What the stone of our self-sufficiency could not do was accomplished by the power of God in the flesh of his son, Jesus, which was derided and then renewed. They wanted to "ensure" his death—and without knowing or believing it—they ensured life for all mankind.

This stone being rolled backwards aroused a variety of feelings. The guards trembled in terror and were "paralyzed as though dead" by their attachment. The women were terrified, but the angel's announcement of life filled them with hope and gave them the gift of joy, a joy that impelled them to run off to spread the news. Death paralyzes; life begs to be communicated.

They are bearers of news: Jesus had not lied, he was alive and they had seen him. The guards, petrified in their existential narrowness, only managed to get as far as the fleeting and circumstantial protection of the payoff. The text continues: "While they were going, behold, some of the guards went into the city and told the chief priests all that had taken place. And when they had assembled with the elders and taken counsel, they gave a sum of money to the soldiers and said, 'Tell people, "His disciples came by night and stole him away while we were asleep." And if this comes to the governor's ears, we will satisfy him and keep you out of trouble.' So they took the money and did as they were directed" (Mt 28:11–15).

Contemplating the contrasting feelings of the women and the guards, we can ask ourselves: Are we here today celebrating the new life that the risen Jesus offers and bestows on us? What appeals to us more, the closed security of the tomb or that happy uncertainty of the angel's announcement? Where is our heart: in the certainty that dead things offered us, without a future, or in that joy in hope of one who is the bearer of news of life? Do we run towards life with the promise of finding it in that Galilee of that encounter, or do we prefer the existential payoff that is guaranteed us by any stone that closes and seals off our heart? Do I prefer sadness or a simple paralyzing satisfaction, or am I encouraged to navigate that path of joy that is born of the conviction that my Redeemer lives?

Before Moses died, he called the people together and told them: "See, I have set before you this day life and good, death and evil" (Dt 30:15). Today, too, in this liturgical celebration close to the risen Jesus truly present on the altar, the Church proposes something similar: Either we believe in the decisiveness of the tomb closed by the stone, adopt it as a way of life, and feed our heart with sadness, or we are encouraged to receive the angel's message: "He is not here, he has arisen," and we take up that gentle and comforting joy of evangelizing which opens the path to proclaiming that he is alive and awaiting us at every moment, in the Galilee of his meeting with each person.

May the Holy Spirit teach us and help us to choose well.

Afraid of Joy?

✑

Homily at the Easter Vigil

BUENOS AIRES, APRIL 7, 2012

At daybreak the women left their house and set out for the tomb. Earlier they had bought perfumes to anoint the body of Jesus. Having prepared everything, they spent nearly the whole night on watch until the sun had risen and there was sufficient light to go out. We, too, are on the watch this night, not preparing ourselves to anoint the body of our Lord but recalling the marvels of God in the history of mankind. We recall especially that God spent the night of that great miracle on watch: "It was a night of watching by the Lord, to bring them out of the land of Egypt" (Ex 12:42). This vigil responds to a mandate of gratitude: "so this same night is a night of watching kept to the Lord by all the people of Israel throughout their generations" (12:42).

Just as with the Israelites, it may be that our children or our acquaintances will ask us about the reason for this vigil. The answer has to arise out of the depths of our memory as a people chosen by God: "By strength of hand the Lord brought us out of Egypt, from the house of bondage" (Ex 13:14). And so it is: "This is the night when the Lord brought from Egypt our fathers, the children of Israel, and allowed them to pass through the Red Sea on foot"; "the night that dispelled the darkness of sins with the splendor of a column of fire" (see Ex 13:21); the night on which we, sinners, are restored to grace; "the night in which Christ broke the bonds of death and rose victorious from the abyss." This is the night in which freedom was secured. For that reason "this night is as clear as day."

With the light of what we celebrate on this vigil, our life goes forward and, as it was for our fathers in the desert, so it will be for us. Many times the difficulties, the distractions on our way, our sorrows and pain, can cloud the joy and even the certainty of that freedom that has been bestowed on us, and we will even come to yearn for the "fine things" that we had in slavery, the garlic and onions of Egypt (see Nm 11:4–6). Impatience might even overcome us and lead us to opt for the idols that are right at hand (see Ex 1–6). At such times, it seems as if the sun has hidden itself, night has come back, and the freedom that we have been given is eclipsed. For Mary Magdalene, Mary the mother of James, and Salome, with the day already begun, they see another night coming upon them, the night of fear, and "they went out and fled from the tomb" (Mk 16:8).

They fled without saying anything to anyone. Fear caused them to forget what they had just heard: "You seek Jesus of Nazareth, who was crucified. He has risen, he is not here" (Mk 16:6). Fear silenced them so they could not proclaim the news. Fear paralyzed their hearts, and they were twisted into feeling sure of complete failure instead of making room for hope—the hope that told them to go to Galilee, where they would see him. And the same thing happens to us: Like them, we are afraid of hope and prefer to hide ourselves away within our limits, pettiness and sins, in doubts and negations which, for good or ill, promise us that we will manage. The women came in mourning to anoint a body, and they stayed that way—just as the disciples of Emmaus were wrapped up in their disillusionment (see Lk 24:13–24). Fundamentally, they were afraid of joy (see Lk 24:41).

And history continues to repeat itself. In our nights of fear, temptation, and trial, nights in which we want to revert to the slavery that has been overcome, God continues to watch as he did on that night in Egypt, and with gentle and fatherly words he tells us: "Why are you troubled, and why do questionings rise in your hearts? See my hands and my feet, that it is I myself; handle me, and see" (Lk 24:38–39). At times he speaks more energetically: "O foolish men, and slow of heart to believe all that the prophets have spoken! Was it not necessary that the Christ should suffer these things and enter into his glory?" (Lk 24:25–26) The risen Lord is always alive at our side.

Every time God showed himself to an Israelite, he tried to calm his fear. Fear not, he would say. Jesus said the same: "Fear not"; "Be not afraid." This is what the angel said to these three women who were full of fear. On this night of vigil, let us say to one another: Have no fear; we are not afraid; we will not try to dodge the certainty that is imposed on us; we will not reject hope. We will not choose the security of the tomb—in this case not empty but filled with the rebellious filth of our sins and egoism. Let us embrace the gift of hope. Let us not fear the joy of the resurrection of Christ.

That night, his mother, too, was watching. Her heart led her to intuit the nearness of that life that she conceived in Nazareth, and her faith strengthened the intuition. We ask her that, as the first disciple, she teach us to remain watching, that she accompany us in patience, strengthen us in hope; we ask that she lead us towards the meeting with her Risen Son; that she free us from fear, so that we can hear the announcement of the angel and also run off, but not out of fear—instead, to announce it to others who need it so much.

CORPUS CHRISTI HOMILIES

The Eucharist: Reclaiming the Memory of His Love

☙

Homily on the Solemnity of Corpus Christi

BUENOS AIRES, JUNE 13, 2009

The reading from chapter 24 of the Book of Exodus tells us of a liturgical dialogue between Moses and the people. Moses read the Law of God, and the people responded and committed themselves: "All the words which the Lord has spoken we will do" (Ex 24:3). Thus the covenant between God and the people was sealed.

In the sacraments, we often take up this dialogue of the covenant, of true commitment. On the day of our baptism, the priest asked our parents: "Are you willing to educate your child in the Faith?" and they responded: "Yes, we are willing." In the sacrament of matrimony all you Christian spouses were asked: "Are you willing to be faithful?" And you answered: "Yes, we are willing." In our ordination, we priests were asked: "Are you willing to preside faithfully over the Eucharist for the praise of God and sanctification of the Christian people?" and we responded: "Yes, we are willing."

Behind those commitments of the covenant, we recognize the style of Jesus, which has remained engraved in the memory of the liturgy: his way of entering our life, always asking permission, asking if we want to receive him. Our Lord always says:

"Behold, I stand at the door and knock; if any one hears my voice and opens the door, I will come in to him and eat with him, and he with me" (Rv 3:20). Jesus does not invade our life. He always asks: "Do you want to walk with me? Are you ready to go a step further?"

Faced with so many realities that either seduce or threaten us, Jesus always appeals, again and again, to our freedom. When his words about the Eucharist seemed hard to many, Jesus himself asked his friends: "And you? Do you also wish to leave me?" And Peter, in the name of all of them said "No, Lord. To whom shall we go?" (Jn 6:68).

In the Eucharist, which Jesus had "ardently desired" (Lk 22:15) to share with us, this dialogue of the covenant attains all of its power in the humility of the Lord's offering. When we listen to him say, "Take and eat," his tone is: "Do you want to eat my flesh and drink my blood?" When he says, "Do this in my memory," he is asking us: "Are you willing to do this in my memory?" This very simple gesture of offering himself as bread is one of unconditional love, a gesture that asks to be received humbly by another love, also unconditional.

It is here that the Eucharist, even if at times we may lay it aside for a while, is always reborn at the important moments of our life. Our Lord accompanies us on the way, even though we don't realize it, and there is always a moment in which, at the breaking of the bread, our eyes are opened and we recover the memory of his love. This is what it is to celebrate the Eucharist: to recover, or reclaim, the memory of his love!

Jesus anticipated in the Eucharist the gift of himself that he was going to carry out on the Cross. He concentrated in the Eucharist all of his love. For this reason, the Eucharist has the power to open our eyes, to make us "remember," to flood the memory of our heart with love. The Eucharist turns us into contemporaries of the mystery of the Cross and resurrection of Jesus. It maintains us in the covenant of love with our Lord until he returns.

Today is a very special day for us to renew our covenant, to feel how our Lord himself is asking us humbly, "Are you willing to relive once more the memorial of my Love?" And we respond together with all our heart, "Yes, we are willing!" Let us do this from our hearts.

Our Lord commanded us to remain in his love, and a grateful memory is a way of doing so. Are you willing to keep the memory of this love from being forgotten? Are you willing to remain in the love of Jesus?

Yes, we are willing!

Our Lord commanded us to forgive one another, and sharing the Eucharist implies forgiving and accepting us. Are you willing to forgive and to let yourself be forgiven?

Yes, we are willing!

Our Lord commanded us to give food to the hungry. Receiving the body of Christ implies the commitment of extending this sharing of bread to all of our brothers and sisters and in all dimensions of life. Are you willing to share?

Yes, we are willing!

Our Lord, in his washing of the feet, commanded us not to distance ourselves from his mercy. Are you willing to let our Lord approach you and touch you with his mercy, to wash your feet and cleanse them?

Yes, we are willing!

Our Lord, on the road to Emmaus, reproached the disciples, who were walking along, shut up in their sad thoughts, lacking in faith, their conscience isolated and separated from the community. Are you willing to let our Lord ignite hope in your heart and make you say as a single people: "Jesus, Lord of history, we need you"?

Yes, we are willing!

Are you willing not to give up, to put out into the deep once more, each morning, and to throw out the nets in his name even though up to now it has seemed you have not caught anything, certain that he will be waiting on the shore with the fire lit and the grilled fish and warm bread that will comfort you after your hard work?

Yes, we are willing!

With these desires, with the consoling tone of this dialogue of love and of the New Covenant, we approach today to receive Communion with devotion. Let us allow the living memory of the Lord to win our heart, anointing with gratitude and hope every corner of our life, especially those places where we have not allowed his light and the forgiving warmth of his mercy to enter.

Thus, fed with this blessed bread and anointed with this saving blood, we will go forth to anoint every last corner of our city. He is sending us as he sent the first seventy-two men and women missionaries, two by two, to the places where he was later to go. We go to announce his coming; we go before him and make room for him. He wants to communicate with our lives; he is thirsty for all that is ours, all that is human, especially for our sins so that he may forgive them. He is hungry for all that happens to us, hungry for our love. Our Lord became the Eucharist because he wanted to enter into communion with us, a communion of love, a communion of friendship.

Let us not lose the memory of this Covenant; let us remain in the memory of the love of Jesus, dismissing every invitation to resentment, hatred, disunion, egoism, and rancor. Let us remain in love, and let us say from the bottom of our hearts that we prefer this path, that we are ready to go forward in this covenant of love. Amen.

The Bread of Life: Accept No Substitutes!

ↄ◌

Homily on the Solemnity of Corpus Christi

BUENOS AIRES, JUNE 5, 2010

The Gospel tells how Jesus began to speak to the people about the kingdom of God and heal the sick. The afternoon was drawing to a close, and the disciples approached to ask him to dismiss the people, as though informing him that the workday was over and it was "quitting time." But Jesus sensed something else: the people were following him just because they wanted to be with him.

We are all moved when someone wants to be with us simply because he loves us. Jesus was touched, too, that the people wanted to stay with him. Simple people intuit what is deepest in God's heart: Jesus is God with us, the God who came to stay in our history. "I am with you always," he says, "to the close of the age" (Mt 28:20). Jesus was happy that the people desired to be with him. He sensed that it is the Father who nourishes this desire in the hearts of men: "No one can come to me, unless the Father who sent me draws him" (Jn 6:44), and "him who comes to me I will not cast out" (6:37).

Of course people wanted him to cure their sick, and everybody liked to hear him tell parables and speak of the kingdom, but more than anything they liked being close to Jesus; they enjoyed spending long periods of time with him. They intuited by faith that he was already the living bread, the bread from heaven that the Father gives us; and they sensed that to be near that bread gave life, life in its fullness. As the Good Shepherd said: "My sheep hear my voice, and I know them, and they follow me; and I give them eternal life" (Jn 10:27–28).

The same thing happens today. People follow Jesus. They don't always come to the ceremonies to which the Church invites them, because an invasive pagan culture tends to devalue our traditions and seeks to replace them. Still, God's faithful people continue to hear the voice of the Good Shepherd and follow him. I like to think that their petitions for bread, for work, for health, besides constituting true needs, are delightful pretexts to be close to Jesus. God's people still truly hunger for the Bread of Life.

When someone acts in a way reminiscent of Jesus, with the bread of gentleness and holiness, people huddle close with devotion. We see this with our own saints: Ceferino, Fr. Brochero, Don Zatti, and Mama Antula. When someone puts Jesus' approach into action, sharing the bread of mercy and solidarity, people sense this and offer their collaboration to those who work to help others.

And where the signs of this bread are—the home and the mother—the signs that God has wished to remain with us, as in Luján, people go there humbly, in great numbers. As we say on the day of Our Lady, in Luján, Mary remained with us so that we would feel that our country has a mother, and to show us that her shrine is the home of the Argentinean people.

Let us follow Jesus there where he reveals himself most of all as our bread, where he makes clear that he wants "to stay with us." The Eucharist is the greatest sign of this ardent desire of his to nourish us, to give us life, to enter into communion with mankind. It is therefore the sacrament of our faith and the proof of his love. We, who have the good fortune to live in this blessed land, we who know good bread when we taste it, must accept no substitute for the true Bread.

- We say *yes* to the Bread of Life—Jesus Christ—and *no* to the substances of death.
- We say *yes* to the bread of truth, and *no* to the blather of empty, banal discourse.
- We say *yes* to the bread of the common good, and *no* to all exclusion and unfairness.
- We say *yes* to the bread of glory, which the risen Jesus broke for us, and no to the pagan vulgarity that leaves the heart empty.

We know that Jesus alone is the Bread of Life. The Father has given him to us. There is only one living and true bread: the One who was born in Bethlehem, grew up in Nazareth, died on Calvary, and arose the next Sunday: Jesus Christ, our Lord. And we want to take responsibility for that bread, for while it is a gift of God, it is also a task for us. The Lord is asking us to help share him out as bread: he wants to be close to the people who need his presence by way of our hands. Jesus Christ, the Bread of Life, wants our assistance as he gives himself to be shared, to be bread to sustain and unite us all around him: our families, and our whole Argentinean people.

Our Lord has not only given himself to us, he has also allowed us to participate in the sweet task of distributing him. And in distributing him, we become community. For bread creates bonds, makes us want to stay on, working together to prepare it and then lingering after the meal to give thanks. The communion that our Lord gave us with the Eucharist is so special that he wanted to leave people in his Church who would consecrate their whole lives to the service of the bread. Priests see to it that the Bread of Life is always within reach of God's people. Let us pray today especially for them, for our pastors, at this end of the Year for Priests. Let us thank them for making Jesus present in the midst of our daily life, in each act of forgiveness, in each anointing, in each Eucharist.

Blessed be the most holy bread from heaven, given to us by our Father! Let us draw near to receive the Bread of Life; let us ask our Lord to remain with us. Let us ask him from our heart: "Lord, give us this bread always."

Let us receive and share the Bread of Life with all our love on this feast of Corpus Christi. Bread received, bread shared. May the Body and Blood of Christ preserve us for eternal life.

Savoring the Joy of Christ

⌒

Homily on the Solemnity of Corpus Christi
BUENOS AIRES, JUNE 25, 2011

In the Gospel we have just heard, our Lord says: "Truly, truly, I say to you, unless you eat the flesh of the Son of Man and drink his blood, you have no life in you" (Jn 6:53). And in the Office of Readings for Corpus Christi there is a very beautiful antiphon that can help us to meditate on this phrase of our Lord. It's from St. Augustine, and it says: "Eat the bond which keeps you united, lest you be scattered; drink the price of your redemption, lest it be devalued" (*Sermon,* 228 B).

Look at what Augustine says: The Body of Christ is the bond that keeps us united. The Blood of Christ is the price he paid to save us: it's the sign of how valuable we are. Therefore, let us eat the Bread of Life that keeps us united as brothers, as a Church, as the faithful people of God. Let us drink the Blood with which our Lord shows how much he loves us. And thus let us remain in communion with Jesus Christ; let us not be scattered, and let us not devalue or despise ourselves.

This invitation also indicates the reality of our hearts because when a person, or a society, suffers dispersion and devaluation, there is undoubtedly a lack of peace and joy in the heart. Sadness sets in instead. Discord and scorn are the offspring of sadness.

Sadness is an evil proper to a worldly spirit. The remedy is *joy*: the joy that only the Spirit of Jesus gives, a joy that nothing and nobody can snatch away.

Jesus brings joy to the people's hearts: that was the announcement of the angels to the shepherds: "Be not afraid; for behold, I bring you good news of a *great joy* which will come to all the people; for to you is born this day in the city of David a Savior, who is Christ the Lord. And this will be a sign for you: you will find a babe wrapped in swaddling cloths and lying in a manger" (Lk 2:10–12).

The salvation that Jesus brought consists in the forgiveness of sins: not a restricted forgiveness ("this far, but no farther!"), but *the joy of forgiveness*. "There will be more joy in heaven over one sinner who repents than over ninety-nine righteous persons who need no repentance" (Lk 15:7). Forgiveness does not end in forgetfulness, nor even in reparation, but in an outpouring of love at the feast arranged by a merciful Father for his returning son.

The social relations which blossom from this joy are relations of justice and peace, not the vengeful justice of an eye for an eye, which appeases hatred but leaves the soul empty and dead, unable to continue life's journey. This is the justice of the kingdom, which radiates from a heart that has succeeded in "receiving the Lord with joy"—like Zacchaeus, who from that abundance decided to return what he had stolen, making ample compensation to the victims of his injustice.

The joy of Jesus' presence is always "catching." If we look at the joy that overpowered the disciples when they saw the risen Lord, we see that it was so great that "they still disbelieved for joy"—and then our Lord asked them for something to eat. He centered that joy on the communion of the table, on sharing. The Pope has a very beautiful reflection: he says that Luke used a special word to speak of how the risen Christ gathered with his own: he gathered them together "eating salt with them." In the Old Testament, joining together to eat bread and salt, or even salt alone, served to seal a solid alliance (Nm 18:19). Salt guarantees durability. The risen Jesus "eating salt" with them is a sign of the incorruptible life he brings us. That salt of life—the consecrated bread shared in the Eucharist—is a symbol of the joy of the Resurrection. Christians share the "salt of life" of the Risen One, and it protects us from corruption, from being dispersed and scorned. But if the salt loses its savor, with what will it be re-salted (see Mt 5:13)?

The joy of the gospel, of forgiveness, of justice! The joy of being companions at table with the Risen One! When we allow the Spirit to gather us together at the table of the altar, his joy will enter deeply into our heart and the fruits of unity and esteem among brothers and sisters will blossom spontaneously in a thousand creative ways.

Let us eat the Bread of Life: it is our bond of union. Let us eat it together, lest we be separated or cut off. Let us drink the Blood of Christ, the price of our redemption, lest we devalue ourselves or despise ourselves!

What a beautiful way of perceiving and tasting the Eucharist! The blood of Christ, which he shed for us, shows us our worth. We sometimes value ourselves mistakenly: at first, we think we're the best in the world; later, we switch to despising ourselves, to feeling that we can't succeed at anything. We swing from one extreme to the other. The Blood of Christ gives us true self-esteem—we're worth a lot in Jesus' eyes! Not because we are better or worse than other people, but because we have been and remain very much beloved.

We're also very prone to the temptation to be at odds with each other, to engage in infighting, to cut ourselves off. Yet, at the same time, a powerful desire for unity remains in our hearts —the desire to be a single people, open to all races and all men and women of good will. Unity is rooted in our heart, and when we cultivate it with dialogue, justice, and solidarity, it becomes a source of great joy. The Eucharist is a font of unity. Let us eat this bread, so that we don't end up dispersed, anarchic, split into a thousand competing subgroups.

Let us ask Mary to guard us against the plague of dispersion and contempt: these are the bitter fruits of sad hearts. Let's ask our Mother, the Cause of our Joy, as one of her most beautiful litanies puts it, to help us to savor the Bread of the Covenant, the Body of her Son, so that we may remain united in the Faith, held together in fidelity, joined in a common hope. Let us ask our Mother to remind Jesus of the times when we "have no wine," so that the joy of Cana will flood our hearts, making us feel how much we are worth, how precious we are in the eyes of the God who did not hesitate to pay the highest price, his blood, shed to save us from all sorrows and evils, and thus to be a source of everlasting joy for us who love him.

Preparing a "Large Room" for the Lord

⏎

Homily on the Solemnity of Corpus Christi
BUENOS AIRES, JUNE 9, 2012

The disciples' question—"Where will you have us go and prepare for you to eat the Passover?"—prompted an unusual response from our Lord: "Go into the city, and a man carrying a jar of water will meet you; follow him, and wherever he enters, say to the householder, 'The Teacher says, Where is my guest room, where I am to eat the Passover with my disciples?'" (Mk 14:12–14) And so it happened! Our Lord had thought it out and prepared it with care. To celebrate the Passover dinner, he chose this large room, carpeted, with everything ready.

How well our Lord prepared things! He made sure his disciples would participate in the preparation of an event as sacred and unique as the Last Supper.

The Eucharist is the life of the Church. It is our life. Consider the Communion that unites us with Jesus when we receive his Body and Blood. Think of the redemptive sacrifice (because what we eat is his "flesh given for us" and what we drink is his "blood poured out for the forgiveness of sins.") Of all this richness of love in the Eucharist, let us focus today on its *preparation*.

Jesus gave great weight to this business of preparing. It is one of the tasks he reserved for himself to do in heaven: ". . . I go to prepare a place for you. And when I go and prepare a place for

you, I will come again and will take you to myself, that where I
am you may be also" (Jn 14:2–3). In this dynamic of "preparing a
place for us in heaven," the Eucharist is already an anticipation of
that place, a pledge of future glory: each time we come together
to eat the Body of Christ, the place where we celebrate becomes
for a while our place in heaven. He takes us with him, and we
remain there. Every place in which the Eucharist is celebrated—
whether it's a basilica, a humble little chapel, or a catacomb—is
an anticipation of our definitive place, heaven, which is the full
communion of all of the redeemed with the Father, Son, and
Holy Spirit.

And so, this evening, on the feast of Corpus Christi: we
sense this. Here we are, in this common place, coming together
where he is present. And he is with us as the Risen One who prepared the meal for his disciples after they had spent the whole
night catching nothing. John tells us that as soon as the disciples
reached the shore, they saw a charcoal fire *prepared* with fish
lying on it, and bread, too (see Jn 21:9). This is the true image
of who Jesus is for us: He who prepares the Eucharist for us each
day. And we are each invited to participate in this task with our
good deeds. This is what the Lord's parables are getting at when
they urge us to "be prepared" for his coming, like "the faithful
and wise servant, whom his master has set over his household, to
give them their food at the proper time" (Mt 24:45).

How beautiful, after receiving Communion, to think of our
life as a prolongation of the Mass, in which we bring the fruit of
our Lord's presence to our family and neighborhood, our stud-
ies and work. It does us good, too, to think of our daily life as a
preparation for the Eucharist, in which our Lord takes all that is
ours and offers it to the Father.

Like the disciples, we can ask Jesus once more today: "Where
do you want us to prepare the Eucharist?" And he will make us

feel that today, too, he has everything prepared. There are many cenacles in our city where our Lord is already sharing his bread with the hungry, and there are many well-prepared places where the light of his Word is lit with his disciples gathered around it. There are many people walking around with their jars of living water, giving the drink of the gospel to a society thirsty for spirit and truth. Many young people have come a long way today, from our parishes to the Cathedral. They come with the offerings and petitions that they have prepared and gathered along their pilgrimage to present them with Christ to God the Father. We see how the Mass has new meaning when we have prepared ourselves and traveled to reach it.

This is precisely where the Corpus Christi procession through the streets of our city, around our Plaza de Mayo, the gathering place of our people, takes on deep meaning and becomes a true call. Jesus prepares a place to be with us: not a static, closed area but a dynamic and open one, like the lake's shore on that morning of the miraculous catch. The place in which our Lord wants us to prepare his Eucharist is our entire country, our city, symbolized in this plaza. Therefore, we have prepared for the Eucharist by walking, as a sign of inclusion, opening up a place so that all can enter, going forth toward every shore of each person's life. In a society with so many zoned-off areas, so many preserves of power, exclusive and excluding sites, we want to prepare a "large room" for our Lord—like this plaza, as big as our city, our native land, the whole world, with room for everyone. This is how the Lord's banquets are—a feast in which the hall, despised by many of those who had been invited, is filled with humble guests who want to participate with joy in the thanksgiving of our Lord.

Walking with our Lord and filling this plaza with love, we embrace our entire country with our faith and hope, and we beg God with a burning desire that he might transform it into a place for the Eucharist, where everyone gives thanks, where all are invited to partake of the Bread of Life, where we can all share and give the best of ourselves for the common good of everybody, especially the most fragile and abandoned. And we will ask him:

- Where, Lord, would you like us to prepare your Eucharist today?
- Where do you want us to walk in an attitude of adoration and of service?
- Where do you want us to open the door for you so that you can break bread for us?
- Whom would you like us to follow, bearers of living water, teachers of the truth?
- Whom do you want us to go out to invite—the poor and sick, the just and sinners—at the crossroads?

With these questions in our hearts and on our lips, after communing with our Lord, we will go out to walk beside Jesus in the Blessed Sacrament, asking Mary for that readiness to set out on a journey and serve which her Son imprinted upon her as soon as he became incarnate in her virginal womb. There is no one better than her to teach us to prepare a beautiful Eucharist, with bread for everyone and no lack of joy, the wine of the Spirit, as in Cana.

Homilies and Addresses for Priests

⊶

Breaking the Flask

Homily at the Chrism Mass
BUENOS AIRES, APRIL 9, 2009

Our Lord enters once more into the synagogue of Nazareth and, with the calm dignity that marked him, describes the truth of his mission: "Today this scripture has been fulfilled in your hearing" (Lk 4:21). He presented himself as anointed and sent: "The Spirit of the Lord is upon me, because he has anointed me to preach good news to the poor. . . ." (4:18) Anointed and sent— anointed in order to anoint. He wishes to share his own royal dignity with us, and today we celebrate the Eucharist, the memorial of his Passion and resurrection, knowing that we too are anointed and sent, anointed in order to anoint.

In the consecration of the chrism we will ask that God the Father deign to bless and sanctify the ointment—a mixture of oil and perfume—so that those whose bodies are to be anointed with it might "feel within them the anointing of divine goodness."

When we are anointed in baptism, confirmation, and holy orders, what the Spirit makes us feel and taste in our own flesh is the caress of the goodness of the Father, rich in mercy, and of Jesus Christ his Son, our Good Shepherd and friend.

Anointed to Anoint

Upon being anointed by the goodness, we are transformed into anointers. *We are anointed in order to anoint.* Anointed in order to anoint God's faithful. Anointed to make every person who comes into this world, everyone who loves the Lord, feel the goodness and tenderness of God. The Father does not want a single one of his little ones to be lost—to miss feeling his goodness.

The power of the Holy Spirit, with which priests, kings, prophets, and martyrs have been anointed, is none other than the power of goodness. It's a goodness that is wanting in power as the world sees it but all-powerful for one who believes in the Cross of Christ, which is "folly to those who are perishing, but to us who are being saved it is the power of God" (1 Cor 1:18).

This balm of divine goodness is not to be hidden, like the talent buried by the servant, nor stored away in its flask. The flasks that will be blessed are to be distributed to all of the churches, to the chrismatory of each priest—and then brought out to touch the vulnerable flesh of the faithful, who need the balm of divine goodness to continue their difficult pilgrimage through this life. Once the bottle is broken, like the flask of aromatic nard with which Mary anointed Jesus' feet, the perfume of God's goodness should reach all God's people with its caresses and its fragrance, that it may fill "the house . . . with the fragrance of the ointment" as St. John says in chapter 12, verse 3, beginning with the smallest and most fragile and spreading out until it reaches everyone. We are anointed to anoint our city with this goodness, in the thousand ways in which it needs and demands it, this city that longs for it.

The physical space of our city needs to be anointed like a new church or altar. Our city needs to be anointed in those places where goodness is lived out naturally, in family homes, schools, maternity hospitals where new life begins—and also where it suffers and ends. These places need to be anointed so that their goodness may be strengthened and spread throughout our society.

Our city also needs to be anointed in those places where goodness is struggling, the ones that seem like a no man's land, which wind up occupied by selfish interests. I'm referring to those places of social and economic injustice, where goodness—the common good—ought to reign. We all want this: it is written as natural law upon the heart of every man and woman. But also, and in a special way, our city needs to be anointed in those places where evil is most intense: places of aggression and violence, chaos, corruption, deceit, and robbery.

Our city's inhabitants need to be anointed. Our children should be sealed as belonging to Christ, our young people with the seal of the Spirit, something they unconsciously long for with all their tattoos that can never satisfy their thirst for a deeper identity. More than for life, our young people yearn for that seal of the Spirit—that visible sign of the name of Christ that is sealed on their heart of flesh, which seeks to reveal itself in a thousand ways. They need and demand loudly that someone anoint them and show them that they belong to Christ, that their masters are not marijuana or cocaine or beer, but Christ their Lord, the One who can summon them, fulfill them, preach the truth to them, and walk beside them.

Our people need priests who are anointers, priests who can leave their complacency and efficiency behind and give of themselves with simple gestures of goodness. Priests who go forth, who know how to get close to people, receiving them warmheartedly, devoting time to them so they will feel that God has time for them, too—caring for them, blessing, forgiving, and healing them. Our people need priests who anoint without an air of messianism or functionalism. Priests who do not store the flask away without breaking it open. Priests who venture out and yet remain close to the tabernacle, who return to it to fill their lamps with oil before going out again.

What is the sign that the oil has not run out, that our anointing has not dried up? The oil with which Jesus was anointed is an *oil of gladness*. The sign that our heart is overflowing with perfumed oil is spiritual joy—the gentle happiness of having worn oneself out with goodness, not for show (complacency) or mere duty (the efficiencies of "God management"). It's a joy mixed with the exhaustion of the patient Christ, the good Christ, who had compassion for his little sheep without a shepherd, staying with them and teaching them for such a long time.

Goodness tires but does not exhaust: it tires because it is toilsome and requires repetition of personal gestures, the ones our faithful people ask for insistently: baptize their babies, anoint their sick, bless their holy cards and bottles of water, visit their homes and hear their confessions, take them Communion. The anointing makes those small gestures of priestly kindness overflow with joy and apostolic efficacy. After all, Jesus' saving strength and power were incarnated and rooted in very simple acts of goodness: blessing bread, laying hands on the sick, teaching the humble the parables of the merciful Father's goodness.

On this day, we renew our priestly anointing. We feel the hand of our Lord upon us, anointing us once more. We feel the intensity and tenderness of his gaze, calling us once again to follow him closely. And, like little children, we ask our Mother, the Blessed Virgin, to give us the grace of recognizing that we are anointed as she was, through the benevolent gaze of the Father, looking at our littleness, able to look upon the little ones of our faithful people and anoint them with goodness and mercy.

No Sheep Without a Shepherd

ℰℰ⌾

Letter to Priests on the Solemnity of Pentecost

BUENOS AIRES, MAY 31, 2009

During these days, from the Ascension to Pentecost, I have reflected a lot on the scattering of the apostles after they received the Holy Spirit. At the moment of ascending to the Father, Jesus announced, "You shall receive power when the Holy Spirit has come upon you; and you shall be my witnesses in Jerusalem and in all Judea and Samaria, and to the end of the earth" (Acts 1:8). Shortly before this, "the apostles whom he had chosen" (Acts 1:2) asked him a self-referential question: "Lord, will you at this time restore the kingdom to Israel?" (Acts 1:6), and our Lord brought them back into the real world ("brought them down with a slingshot," as we say in Buenos Aires): "It is not for you to know times or seasons which the Father has fixed by his own authority" (Acts 1:7). This way of situating someone in concrete reality is very characteristic of Jesus. Recall how he puts Peter in his place when he tries to satisfy his curiosity about the life of John: "If it is my will that he remain until I come, what is that to you?" (Jn 21:22). In the end, the apostles were faithful, and they let themselves be led all over by the Holy Spirit, reading the signs of God in the most diverse circumstances; one need only read the Acts of the Apostles attentively to see it.

When, during these days between the Ascension and Pentecost, I have been struck by the dispersion of the apostles, it occurred to me that it was "charged" for me by our fraternal dialogue with the bishops of the country a week earlier, in the Assembly. Listening to their presentations, talking about the reality of their respective dioceses, I became aware once more of so many difficulties that we here in the capital don't deal with. The main one is the lack of priests to attend to their communities. There are extensive dioceses with only 10 or 15 percent as many priests as we have. The situation of a parish priest with various towns under his care, and not exactly next to each other, either, is not a rare situation.

I share these sentiments with you to ask you to take into account this "sign of the times" in our country. Our Lord unites us in one body, and we are also touched to some degree by concern for all of our churches. I would like to ask you, in all simplicity and a friendly spirit, for each of you to allow apostolic generosity to grow and, with the love of a disciple, take courage to ask our Lord: "What do you want me to do?" It is a matter of opening our hearts, letting Jesus look at us, and asking him for grace to see that great multitude, like sheep without a shepherd (see Mk 6:34), and have compassion on them as he did. It is possible that, upon asking him the question, there might come as a temptation some self-interested thought. Let it be our Lord himself who dispels it, as he did for Peter and the apostles; let him send his angels as he did on the day of the Ascension, asking them: "Why do you stand looking into heaven?" (Acts 1:11). We can then turn to look at those who are "like sheep without a shepherd."

I ask you to forgive me for this meddling in your lives, but I feel certain that I am doing it from a heart that has been moved this past week with the desire to serve the Church. From now on, I thank each of you for your fervent prayer for these brother churches in need of clergy, and also for the availability with which you consider this before our Lord. Would that some of you might sense his call to follow him toward those places!

Please, I ask you to pray for me. May Jesus bless you, and the Holy Virgin care for you.

The Source of Priestly Stamina

cʖᴏ

Homily at the Chrism Mass

BUENOS AIRES, APRIL 1, 2010

"The Spirit of the Lord is upon me, because he has anointed me."—LUKE 4:18

My dear brother priests, last year at this same Eucharist, we reflected on the *aim* of the priestly ministry: *anointed in order to anoint.* The priest is there for the faithful, for all who need to be anointed with the mercy and charity of our Father God. We need the anointing of the Spirit that makes us walk together with the people of God in the acknowledgement of Jesus Christ as our one Savior and Lord. We need it in a very special way in these times of such great material poverty, with our faith so much under siege.

Today I want to invite you to contemplate the *source* from which the anointing comes, to fix your eyes on the Spirit that reposes upon Christ the priest, the Spirit of holiness in which we were consecrated through our priestly anointing. Let us contemplate the Father, font of all holiness, who sent the Spirit upon his beloved Son. The Spirit signs the head, the heart, and the hands of Jesus with the seal of anointing and consecrates him as priest forever. At that same fount our priestly ministry has its origin. The same Spirit who anointed our Lord has consecrated us priests through this anointing.

Let us look with eyes of faith upon Christ anointed by the Spirit—Christ the shepherd pastured by the Spirit and Christ the leader led by the Spirit that the Father sent to descend upon him, who accompanied him throughout his whole life, anointing every one of his actions and also those of every person he chose to send.

This Spirit who is over our Lord and whom he obeyed, allowing himself to be led, is also over us, guiding and leading us from within. It is not flesh or blood that guides us on our journey as pastors. Nor is it human prudence or personal advantage that moves us here or there. The Spirit is the one who inspires our actions, and he does it for the praise and glory of God and for the good of his faithful people.

This Spirit imprinted a character on our own spirit when the bishop laid hands on us and prayed, asking God to "renew in their hearts the Spirit of holiness." With him we are joined in each Eucharist when we extend our hands over the offering of bread and wine and say to the Father, fount of all holiness: "Make holy, therefore, these gifts, we pray, by sending down your Spirit upon them." It is this Spirit that we invoke so that through us he may transmit the grace of baptism on children, forgiveness on penitents, and anointing on the suffering of the sick.

Through Christ, with him, and in him, we can repeat: "The Spirit of the Lord is upon me, because he has anointed me." It is comforting to chant these words, as a psalm of faith, attentive to the fount of grace and not only to its purpose. When we focus on those to whom we are sent, although there is great consolation in seeing the good they receive through our ministry, what comes first is pastoral fatigue: the harvest is great and we laborers are few (see Mt 9:37). There is always good to be done; we always need more; the Cross is always present in our daily work. On the other hand, when we look at the source from which the grace of our ministry comes, at the giver more than the recipients, consolation blossoms forth freely and superabundantly. The fount of living water never runs dry, the fire of his love is never extinguished, and neither is the breath of his inspirations, which enlighten our mind and set our hands and feet in evangelical motion.

Christ Provides the Energy

Where did the untiring energy of the apostles, saints, and martyrs come from? Where was it nourished, that apostolic zeal and inexhaustible patience that allowed them to endure all things and hope all things (see 1 Cor 13:7)? It blossomed forth from the patience and gentleness of Christ, the distinctive form of their holy priesthood, to which all undue fatigue, aggression, and tension are foreign. And where was this sweet shepherding of Christ nourished, which is communicated to his priests the moment we extend our hand, as soon as we rest in his pierced side, as we bend down a little to consecrate? This patience, sweetness, gentleness, and priestly stamina are all nourished by the Spirit and his anointing. We anoint others when we allow ourselves to be anointed by the Spirit of Christ, meek and humble of heart (see Mt 11:29); when we submerge ourselves in him and allow him to permeate our pastoral wounds, the ones that wear on our minds and stress our nerves.

We are called to be stones, it is true, but anointed stones. Hard as rock on the outside, to build and sustain, to protect the flock and shelter it, but not hard or tense within. Within the priest it must be like the oil in the flask, the fire in the lamp, the wind in the sails, the crumbs of bread.

In order to anoint, we must seek diligently and receive abundantly the anointing of the Spirit in every corner of our soul, so that grace may reach the depths, superabundant and ready to be poured out on others.

We are poor priests in the Great Priest, little shepherds in the Great Shepherd. The grace that passes through our lips and hands is infinitely greater than we can imagine, and the oil of the anointing is what makes us good leaders—leaders who are led.

Priestly Gentleness

The sign of being leaders who are led is *growth in priestly gentleness*. The anointing entails the Spirit's gentle appropriation of our whole being for the anointing of others. We have the beautiful image of this grace in the "Patient Christs" that our people love so much. Our faithful are tired of a world of aggression, of brothers against brothers, destruction and calumny. Our people do not want priests who are on edge. And edginess comes from trying to control one's own power. This is precisely the opposite of the good pastor's knowledge that he himself is being led. Our faithful people are asking us for *patience* and *gentleness.*

Priestly gentleness is the sign of a heart that knows itself to be guided and led: "Thy rod and thy staff, they comfort me" (Ps 23:4). Gentleness and priestly patience are signs of a heart that knows itself to be blessed, defended, consoled, sent into the midst of its people to form a covenant, anointed by the same Spirit who anointed the beloved Son, the one priest and Good Shepherd of the sheep.

We are now approaching the conclusion of the Year for Priests. May the greatest homage to our priesthood for others be to allow the Spirit to renew our anointing in the depths of our soul, full and superabundant, so that without taking our eyes off those for whose service we have been anointed, we will rejoice in heart, freely, in the one who gives himself to us in his gift.

Anointed with the Oil of Gladness

ൟ

Homily at the Chrism Mass
BUENOS AIRES, APRIL 21, 2011

Each Holy Thursday, at the Chrism Mass, we return to the eternal present of this scene, in which St. Luke symbolically sums up our Lord's entire ministry. We gather, as if around a fountain, to hear the words of Christ, who tells us that the Scripture we have just heard has been fulfilled today (see Lk 4:21).

The Lord makes his own that text from Isaiah in order to instruct us about himself and his mission. In his humility he does not even use his own words, but simply takes up what was prophesied by this very beautiful text, a continuation of the "Book of Consolation."

As priests, we participate in the same mission that the Father entrusted to his Son, and therefore, at each Chrism Mass, we come to renew the mission, to reawaken in our hearts the grace of the spirit of holiness that our mother the Church communicates through the laying on of hands. It is the same Spirit that rested on Jesus, the supreme priest and beloved Son, and which today rests on all the priests of the world, sending us out to preach in the midst of God's faithful people. In the name of Jesus we have been sent to preach the truth, to do good to everyone, and to bring joy to the lives of our people. Our mission is deployed at once in these three areas. In the first two, it is obvious: Every proclamation of the gospel is always translated into some concrete act of teaching, mercy, and justice—but not only as an obligatory action following reflection. In the very heart of the gospel truth, it is love that gives light, and the truth that shines most brightly in our Lord's parables is the mercy of a Father waiting for his prodigal son. This is the truth that impels one to go out of oneself with the compassionate heart of the Good Shepherd, the truth that does good. The third area, that of joy and the glory which is the beauty of God, requires that we dedicate a moment of reflection to "tasting and seeing" the beauty of our mission.

St. Luke sums up this beauty of the servant's mission with the image of being able to live a "year of grace." Let us imagine for a moment what that meant for a people in the constant turmoil of violence and injustice to be able to live one year peacefully, a year of celebration and harmony. The prophet Isaiah describes the beauty of this mission with three delightful images that revolve around the word "console." We are sent to "console the afflicted, the afflicted of our people." This consolation consists in exchanging ashes for a crown, mourning clothes for the oil of gladness, and dejection for a song of praise. The prophet speaks of the "garland" of glory in place of "ashes," of "the oil of gladness," and the "mantle of praise" in place of a "faint spirit" (see Is 61:1–3).

A Spirit of Joy and Consolation

Joy and consolation are the fruit (and therefore the gospel sign) that truth and charity are not opposed but are present and operative in our hearts as pastors and in the heart of the people to whom we are sent. When there is joy in the heart of the pastor, it is a sign that his actions come from the Spirit. When there is joy in the people, it is a sign that what is reaching them—as a gift and proclamation—is of the Spirit. For the Spirit is a spirit of consolation, not bitterness.

Let us feel and relish these images of Isaiah for a moment. Imagine the people as they are on feast days, dressed in their best clothes, their eyes lit up by the brightness of the flowers adorning the images of Our Lady and the saints, singing and blessing God with reverence and an inner joy. How well these scenes depict the spirit with which Jesus indicates that he dwells in the midst of his people! The signs are not merely decorative. They constitute the essence of the mission, the "the gentle and comforting joy of evangelizing" that Paul VI mentioned, so that "today's world—which searches at times anxiously, at times hopefully—can receive the Good News, not through sad and discouraged evangelizers, impatient or anxious (the spirit of sloth), but through ministers of the Gospel whose life ignites the fervor of those who have received, first of all within themselves, the joy of Christ" (*Aparecida*, 552).

It is not enough that our truth be orthodox and our pastoral action efficient. Without the joy of beauty, the truth becomes cold, even heartless and arrogant, as we see in the speech of many embittered fundamentalists. It is as if they were chewing on ashes instead of savoring the glorious sweetness of Christ's truth, which illuminates all of reality with a gentle glow, accepting it as it is each day.

Without the joy of beauty, any work for the good becomes a gloomy concern for efficiency, as it is for many overwhelmed activists. They go about clothing reality with mournful statistics instead of anointing it with the oil of inner gladness that transforms hearts, one by one, from within.

A spirit of sour and gloomy *acedia* is the opposite of our Lord's spirit of consolation. This spirit soaks everything with the vinegar used by both embalmers of the past and anxious imaginers of the future. It is one and the same spirit, and it may be recognized by the way it tries to rob us of the *joy of the present*: the *poor joy* of one who is content with what our Lord gives him each day, the *fraternal* joy of one who enjoys sharing what he has, the *patient joy* of simple, hidden service, the *hopeful joy* of letting oneself be led by our Lord in today's Church. When Jesus says, "Today this scripture has been fulfilled in your hearing," it is an invitation to the joy and consolation of God's "today." Notice that was the first thing that appeared as grace in the hearts of those who, St. Luke tells us, bore witness and marveled at the words of grace that came from his mouth. But this consolation is no passing emotion: it is the choice of a life's direction. Jesus' fellow villagers opted for listlessness, acedia: "He speaks well, but why doesn't he do here among us what they say he did in Capernaum?" Here we see the universal mission of the servant reduced to a local squabble between Nazareth and Capernaum. Internal squabbles in the Church are always the daughters of sadness, and they always generate even more sadness.

When I say that consolation is a choice, we must understand clearly that it is a choice open to the poor and the little ones, not the conceited or grandiose. It is the choice of a shepherd who trusts in the Lord and goes forth to announce the gospel without a staff or an extra pair of sandals, who follows peace—that stable and constant form of joy—wherever our Lord leads him.

This Spirit of consolation is not only present before we set out as missionaries. It also awaits us, with its abundant joy, in the midst of the mission, in the heart of the people of God. And if we look carefully, when it comes to joy, what we stand to receive surpasses what we have to give. How our faithful people rejoice when they see that they can give joy to us! How happy they are when we rejoice with them! This is simply because they need pastors who are themselves comforted, who allow themselves to be consoled so that they lead not in complaint or anxiety but in praise and serenity; not in a state of tension but in the patience that comes with the anointing of the Spirit.

May Our Lady, who receives in abundance the consola tions of our people—who, like Elizabeth, are constantly telling her, "Blessed are you who believed!" "Blessed are you among women!" and "Blessed is the fruit of your womb, Jesus!"—help us participate in this spirit of consolation so that our proclama tion of the truth may be joyful, and our works of mercy anointed with the oil of jubilation.

Remain in the Anointing

乀◎

Homily at the Chrism Mass
BUENOS AIRES, APRIL 5, 2012

Psalm 89 speaks of the "forever" of the anointing: "I have found David, my servant; with my holy oil I have anointed him; so that my hand shall ever abide with him. . . ." The anointing of our Lord is "the fidelity and love which accompanies us" throughout our priestly life. Perhaps it was St. John who best expressed this permanent character of the anointing: "The anointing which you received from him abides in you and you have no need that any one should teach you" (1 Jn 2:27).

The anointing remains in us, but we must remain in it: "As his anointing teaches you about everything, and is true, and is no lie, just as it has taught you, abide in him" (2:27). Abide in the anointing—this teaches us from within how to remain in friendship with Jesus.

We would do well to ask ourselves: What helps us to remain in the anointing? How do we *experience* its joy; how do we *feel* it strengthening us, making the cross mild and bearable; how do we *live* it as a shield against temptation and a balm for wounds? What helps us to keep it from diminishing, from losing its salt, keeping its fervor? How can we avoid lengthening the list of those who have ended badly, who failed to remain anointed: Saul, Esau, Solomon? A little earlier in the same letter, John gives the key: "He who says he abides in him ought to walk in the same way in which he walked" (1 Jn 2:6).

Remaining anointed, then, does not mean mimicking a holy card figure, remaining inert; it means "*to walk,*" and the walking of which John speaks (*periepatesen*) is that of all the paralytics in the Gospel who were cured, who jumped up and walked with their stretchers on their backs, following our Lord. It is Peter's walk towards Jesus, on the water, a symbol of a man walking by faith, who "abandons all security and advances to the encounter that one can only attain by grace" (von Balthasar). To stay anointed, one needs to get up and *walk as Christ walked.*

Walk as Christ Walked

The anointing of the Spirit remained upon our Lord, who "went about doing good," pouring out the Father's mercy upon all who needed it on every occasion, up until the consummation of his Pasch, his exodus from his very self, when his heart was pierced on the Cross. Staying anointed means going about doing good; a good that is not a tangible possession but diffused like the perfume of pure nard with which Mary anointed our Lord. This annoyed Judas, who had lost his anointing and with it his ability to enjoy the fragrance that permeated the whole house. The intangibility of the Spirit's anointing is usually replaced, when lost, by the tangibility of hard cash. Consider the self-referential accounting mentality of so many people and institutions within the Church. What is the state of their anointing? When the people in the desert grew tired of their anointing, they made a golden calf (see Ex 32:1–6).

Remaining anointed is defined in the walking and the doing. This doing is not only deeds, but also a style like that of Jesus. "I have become all things to all men, that I might by all means save some" (1 Cor 9:22) expresses the same idea. The anointed seek to participate in that anointing, in the gentle and humble beating of our Lord's heart, filled with joy at how the Father does everything well and reveals his secrets to the little ones; the anointing that covered his whole body in the Passion so that his wounds, soothed with the medicine of charity, became healing wounds—the oil of gladness of the Resurrection that shines through in the task of consoling one's friends.

But it is precisely in his way of announcing and defending the truth that we can best contemplate his "style," his approach. What stands out most of all is the *patience* our Lord showed in his teaching. His patience with the people (the evangelists show us how he spent hours teaching and conversing with them, even though he was tired); his patience with his disciples (explaining the parables when they were alone, the good humor with which he got them to confess that they had been arguing about which of them was most important, preparing them for his Cross, so that they would recognize him later in the incredible joy of the Resurrection).

The most delightful image, perhaps, is the pilgrimage to Emmaus. The disciples talked and talked, and Jesus listened patiently, making them feel and taste within themselves how good it was *to walk in his company*. When he made as if to continue on, they didn't want him to leave, and he moved them to invite him to stay. Then "their eyes were opened" and they recognized him in the breaking of the bread—this comforting way he had of breaking bread and passing it out to them. In the Eucharist this anointing remains engraved on the Church's memory, one in which each of us, as priests, participates. In the common formula of the Church, each one places what is closest to his heart into the consecration, and it is usually a participated grace from some other priest that allows him to sense the Lord's

anointing. Stay anointed; stay and listen to the Word like one
who shares his bread.

The Grace of Anointed Words

Leave aside for the moment our Lord's keenness and wit, his way
of drawing doctrine out of the most ordinary things, as well as his
masterful elaboration of the parables, even while being tested by
the intelligentsia. Let us contemplate how our Lord's anointing
was revealed in his approach to combating error and the snares
of his enemies. Our Lord never "ran off at the mouth." Though
perfectly capable of being sarcastic (and with good reason), or
indignant, or scathing, his refusal to dialogue with the devil, his
mastery of the tongue with the scribes and Pharisees, his silence
before the powerful, his refusal to retaliate against the weak
who had been infected by their leaders' malice and kicked him
when he was down, all speak of the Anointed One's approach, in
which we are invited to participate. This whole "negative" aspect
of self-dominion is the necessary counterpart to that good word
that is sowed deep in the heart of the humble. The Anointed
One whom we follow does not impose himself on anybody with
arrogant outbursts, nor by mistreating his faithful. He who is the
Word anoints by penetrating gently into the interior of those of
good will and shielding their hearts so that no word of his can be
misused by the enemy.

Today, perhaps more than ever, we need this grace of anointing by words. We need to hear anointed words, which allow us
to internalize the truth with no fear of losing our freedom by
obeying Our Lord's words or those of the Church. The anointed
word instructs us from within. We also need to hear anointed
words that make us "allergic" to all evil ones, those that leave
a foul taste in the mouth and embitter the heart. Our faithful

people need us to preach anointed words, which reach their hearts and make them burn as our Lord's words did with the hearts of the disciples of Emmaus, anointed words that defend the heart from being infiltrated by so many evil words, so much gossip and vulgarity, so many lies and self-interested words. Such talk, heard constantly on all sides today, are the ones that attack and often destroy one's anointing.

Anointed in the Anointed One, we look today to our Mother and ask her to watch over our hearts' anointing. We beg her to look after our eyes and hands so that, with that way of hers, so much like her Son's (which she at first taught to him and later, as a disciple, learned from him), speaks the truth to us and does so—like the good Maccabean woman—in that motherly language (see 2 Mc 7:21, 27). This leads us irresistibly to remain in Jesus. May her goodness help us to understand that anointing is expressed, not in a stiff and artificial pose, but in going about as he did. She will help us to speak and look and work like someone who has been anointed. We ask her that there may never come from our mouths an unedifying word but that, as we keep and ponder in our heart the things concerning her Son, words will spring forth from us to give joy to the faithful, holy people of God, following the footsteps of the Anointed One who came to announce the Good News to them.

Homilies and Addresses
for Bishops

The Spirit of Truth

ego

Homily at the Opening Mass of the 97th Episcopal Assembly

PILAR, MAY 11, 2009

In the mood of farewell before his Passion, Jesus announced "the promise of the Father" (Acts 1:4). "These things I have spoken to you, while I am still with you. But the Counselor, the Holy Spirit, whom the Father will send in my name, he will teach you all things, and bring to your remembrance all that I have said to you" (Jn 14:25–26); and he promises "the Spirit of truth, whom the world cannot receive, because it neither sees him nor knows him; you know him, for he dwells with you, and will be in you"(Jn 14:17). Then, before departing for heaven, he advises them to remain in Jerusalem and wait for the Holy Spirit, for they will be baptized in him and receive his strength, which will make them "witnesses in Jerusalem and in all of Judea and Samaria and to the ends of the earth" (Acts 1:4–8).

We receive these words of Jesus with an open and willing heart. We want our episcopal ministry to be guided by the anointing of the Holy Spirit, and we pray for one another in a special way in this Eucharist.

Transcending the Spirit of the World

Jesus calls the Holy Spirit the "Spirit of Truth." His presence in our hearts dispels the darkness of lies, of those pseudo-truths,

114

half-truths, expressions of compliance, expressions of commitment to the world, who "cannot receive [the Holy Spirit], because it neither sees him nor knows him" (Jn 14.17); expressions generated in the spirit of spiritual worldliness, "the greatest danger, the most perfidious temptation, that which always reemerges insidiously when all the others have been overcome, even being fostered by these same victories. . . . If this spiritual worldliness were to invade the Church and work to corrupt it by attacking it at its very origin, this would be infinitely more disastrous than any other sort of simply moral worldliness. Even worse than the infamous leprosy that, in certain moments of history, has so cruelly disfigured the beloved Bride when gratification seemed to bring the scandal into her very sanctuary."[1]

"Spiritual worldliness is nothing more than a self-centered attitude . . . a subtle humanism, an enemy of the Living God—and, in secret, no less an enemy of man that can install itself within us by a thousand deceits" (de Lubac). When a priest begins negotiating with this attitude he is no longer a shepherd of the people but has become a "career cleric," a state functionary.

The Holy Spirit allows us to transcend and escape the spirit of "this world" that is far more dangerous to its friends than its enemies. This frees us from this trap that lends our ministry a worldly quality. From within, the Holy Spirit leads us and guides us in two different directions: *inwardly*, as we enter into the mystery, and *outwardly*, to give us the strength to witness.

Memory and Teaching

Jesus sends us the Spirit of Truth from the Father, to teach us all things and recall to us what the Lord himself has told us—memory

1. Cardinal Henri de Lubac, *Meditaciones sobre la Iglesia* (Pamplona: Desclée, 2nd ed.), 367–368.

and teaching. The anointing of the Spirit reminds us of doctrine and continues to teach us, disclosing the truth more and more fully as our life unfolds. He urges us towards mystery and initiates us into it. He doesn't forsake us halfway but defends us from turmoil, leading us towards the fullness and maturity of faith. Thus he saves us, as a community of believers, from becoming a gnostic Church, since the knowledge we gain is imbued with wisdom and love. It's a knowledge that anoints us as disciples of Jesus Christ, not simply students of a certain philosophy or doctrine.

But his work in us is not limited to this: he also urges us out into the world, the same world that would not receive the Lord, that hated him and will hate us also (see Jn 15:18–19). He leads us there to bear witness to the resurrection of Jesus. We did not receive the Holy Spirit for ourselves alone, to fuel a spirituality of complacency. We did not we receive him so that our communities might be sole proprietors of the truths they recall. The Spirit goes further and sends us out from within the mystery in which he immerses us. He saves us from being a self-referential Church. He makes us missionaries.

Jesus asks his disciples to remain in Jerusalem until the coming of the gift from the Father. Likewise, he instructs us neither to penetrate further into the mystery by which we are anointed as disciples, nor into the world to bring the Good News as missionary witnesses, until we are driven by the anointing of the Holy Spirit. Knowing how to discern the paths where the Spirit leads and be obedient to him is a grace for our ministerial service that we must beg for daily.

Driven by the Spirit

Our Lady knew this. The Holy Spirit had come upon her (Lk 1:35), and in light of his anointing she kept and pondered all these things in her heart (Lk 2:19, 2:33, 2:51). She never lost the ability to wonder with the astonishment that the Spirit's presence awakens. She never stopped halfway but persevered to the end.

Nor did Paul stop halfway in his dealings with the people of Lystra, seeking some compromise that might allow him to accept worldly honor while still proclaiming Jesus Christ. He reached the end because he was driven by the Spirit of Truth. If we look at John the Baptist, we find the same thing: no bargaining with the worldly vanity of the moment (Jn 1:19–27). Paul's and John's lives bear witness to the Spirit who encourages and brings his work to its fulfillment and consummation. Even Jesus had to endure the commotion of all those who were proposing a "worldly redemption" through wealth, vanity, and power (cf. Mt 4:1–11). He, who was anointed Lord of all, marks the course. He wished to endure the temptation to compromise and overcome it by the power of the Word of God. And he did so because "He was guided by the Spirit" (Mt 4:1, Mk 1:12), "filled with the Holy Spirit," and "led by the Spirit" (Lk 4:1).

We begin this Assembly strengthened by Jesus' promise: "the Counselor, the Holy Spirit, whom the Father will send in my name, he will teach you all things, and bring to your remembrance all that I have said to you." And we pray that this presence of the Spirit may be fully accepted and welcomed into our hearts. Let us allow him to introduce us into the mystery, to send us as witnesses, so as never to invent a gnostic or self-referential church. And so we may reach the finish line without negotiating any shortcuts with the "prudence" of this world, a prudence born of compromises with wealth, vanity, and pride. Our faithful people are asking for pastors, witnesses of the mystery, sent to proclaim Jesus Christ.

True Shepherds Who Nurture the Encounter with God

⸦⸧

Homily at the Opening Mass of the 98th
Assembly of the Episcopal Conference
PILAR, NOVEMBER 9, 2009

The Church, in this commemoration of the primatial cathedral, brings us to the contemplation of the temple as a place of God's presence, source of blessings and fruitfulness in our faith. In Ezekiel, through the figure of the water flowing from the temple, we are told of the life and abundance that flows from the strength of the Lord when it is welcomed by his people. "And on the banks, on both sides of the river, there will grow all kinds of trees for food. Their leaves will not wither nor their fruit fail, but they will bear fresh fruit every month, because the water for them flows from the sanctuary. Their fruit will be for food, and their leaves for healing" (Ez 47:12). The prophet Jeremiah calls blessed the man who trusts in the Lord, who places his confidence in him (see Jer 17:7). "He is like a tree planted by water, that sends out its roots by the stream, and does not fear when heat comes, for its leaves remain green, and is not anxious in the year of drought, for it does not cease to bear fruit" (Jer 17:8). The same blessing is found in Psalm 1:3, directed to the "man who walks not in the counsel of the wicked, nor stands in the way of sinners, nor sits in the seat of scoffers; but his delight is in the law of the Lord, and on his law he meditates day and night" (Ps 1:1–2).

The Blessing and the Curse

The blessing falls upon the man who is open to God, who plants himself firmly in the life-giving stream flowing from the temple, accepting the law and guarding it in his heart. He trusts in the Lord and is therefore freed from fear and anxiety in midday heat and drought; he has no need of those other props that are alien to God and would lead him to place his trust in mankind and seek support in the flesh. The Word of God tells us simply that those who do so are "cursed." The blessing and the curse point to the relationship we have with the temple as a place of God's presence, the site of the encounter with him. Jesus calls it a "house of prayer" (Mt 21:13), a house of dialogue with God, and an encounter with the Lord.

The path of God's people regarding their relationship with the temple has oscillated throughout history between these two poles of the blessing and the curse. The prophets will often denounce their superficial and even superstitious religion, gestures devoid of a right intention: "What to me is the multitude of your sacrifices? says the Lord" (Is 1:11). They complain of evil priests who have bastardized the divine service and profaned the temple: "Many shepherds have destroyed my vineyard, they have trampled down my portion" (Jer 12:10). God's word is very harsh when describing the corruption of priests in the service of the temple. The sons of Eli are one example: they "were worthless men; they had no regard for the Lord" (1 Sm 2:12). Because of their evil ministry, the temple of the Lord became a house of all sorts of profane depravity, which in the end is nothing but idolatry—hence the call of conscience to the faithful Israelite to purify the temple. The sanctuary had grown desolate; the glory of God had departed from it.

Cleansing the Temple

In today's Gospel, Jesus takes charge of this whole tradition of the purification of the temple with a decisive and prophetic gesture. He uses not merely words but concrete deeds—we might even say *craftsmanship*: "And making a whip of cords, he drove them all, with the sheep and oxen, out of the temple; and he poured out the coins of the money-changers and overturned their tables. And he told those who sold the pigeons, 'Take these things away; you shall not make my Father's house a house of trade'" (Jn 2:15–16). With his gestures and his words, he proclaims his Father's house a meeting place for God and his people, cleansing it of all types of material and spiritual trade.

At other times he condemns as hypocrites the ministers who sophisticatedly adulterate the purity of God's house. He confronts them, for they "bind heavy burdens, hard to bear, and lay them on men's shoulders; but they themselves will not move them with their finger. They do all their deeds to be seen by men; for they make their phylacteries broad and their fringes long, and they love the place of honor at feasts and the best seats in the synagogues, and salutations in the market places, and being called rabbi by men" (Mt 23:4–7). He clearly calls them an impediment to the people's encounter with God: they "shut the kingdom of heaven against men; for [they] neither enter [themselves], nor allow those who would enter to go in" (Mt 23:13). "You tithe mint and dill and cumin, and have neglected the weightier matters of the law, justice and mercy and faith" (Mt 23:23). Jesus chases them out with a whip because they desecrate the temple and, with their clerical hypocrisy, stand in the way of their people's encounter with their Lord. They are not men of God; they are only worldly.

Protecting the Encounter

We as pastors are asked to encourage and protect this encounter. We are called to be men of prayer and penance so that our faithful can encounter God: men aware of their call, with attitudes of humility and service. And today, as we begin this Assembly, we pray together for one another. Our people want shepherds dedicated to caring for their encounter with God, and we know full well that in this work of the kingdom we are beset by many temptations of worldliness. I shudder each time I read St. Gregory the Great's view of pastoral ministry:

> There is something else about the life of the shepherds, dearest brothers, which discourages me greatly. But lest what I claim should seem unjust to anyone, I accuse myself of the very same thing, although I fall into it unwillingly—compelled by the urgency of these barbarous times. I speak of our absorption in external affairs; we accept the duties of office, but by our actions we show that we are attentive to other things. We abandon the ministry of preaching and, in my opinion, are called bishops to our detriment, for we retain the honorable office but fail to practice the virtues proper to it. Those who have been entrusted to us abandon God, and we are silent. They fall into sin, and we do not extend a hand of rebuke (Homily 17, 14; *PL* 76, 1146).

When we read this, if the shoe fits, we do what we can to repent, and we hope that there's no rope nearby with which Jesus can fashion a whip. While we all know ourselves to be sinners, we sincerely desire to serve the Lord and his holy, faithful people. We are weak, but we want to open our hearts to the Lord's mercy every day to better serve the encounter between God and his people, to strive to keep open the doors of the temple from which the saving and living waters flow.

The Aparecida conference calls on us to encounter the living Christ and serve our faithful people in that encounter. This must be at the heart of our pastoral conversion, which distances us from the stale old attitudes that prevent our people's entry into the temple. Jesus calls us to shepherd his people, and, if we ask him, he will deliver us from the temptation to become worldly "career clerics." He walks with us and enters the temple with us, and in his company we are confident that we will not be thrown out. And with him is his Mother. We beg her to "teach us to get out of ourselves and set out on the way of sacrifice, love, and service, as she did during the visitation to her cousin Elizabeth, so that as pilgrims along the way we may sing the wonders that God has done for us according to his promise" (*Aparecida*, 553). Amen.

The Shepherd as Little Child

cℛ☉

In the Synoptic Gospels, Jesus' words on scandal refer to the little ones of the kingdom. In this text we just heard, "little ones" refers to the faithful people of God. In Matthew's version (Mt 18: 6–7), he speaks of "the little ones who believe in me" (18:6). The expression is occasioned by the disciples' question about who is the greatest in the kingdom of heaven (18:1). Jesus calls a little child and places him among them, assuring them that if they do not become like children, they will not enter the kingdom: "He who humbles himself like this child, he is the greatest in the kingdom of heaven" (18:4). St. Mark adds a very significant "little ones who have faith" (9:42). Without forcing the meaning, we can understand that Jesus refers to scandal caused to simple believers who are like the children he sets up as models of greatness in discipleship.

These words of Jesus remind me of that encouraging promise in the midst of the terrible "*Dies irae*" of Zephaniah (1:14–18): "For I will leave in the midst of you a people humble and lowly. They shall seek refuge in the name of the Lord" (3:12). Those people, though sinful, were repentant and humble of heart: precisely the little ones, who, just like children, cast aside all pretension and self-sufficiency and put their strength and hope in

123

the Lord and in those who trust in him, abandoning themselves "like a child quieted at its mother's breast" (Ps 131:2).

A Childlike Faith

There is, then, a unique strength within the smallness the Lord asks of us: the strength of our confidence in his power over every eventuality. This persistent and trusting abandonment may sometimes seem ridiculous, even gauche. Hannah, begging God in distress for a son, was mistaken for a drunkard by Eli, the priest (1 Sm 1:14), but she knew perfectly well in whom she had placed her trust, and the strength of her religious understanding was precisely the Lord, faithful to his people. God seeks not a childish faith (which St. Paul condemns in 1 Corinthians 3:1–3, 14:20) but a childlike one, an awareness of one's weakness, expressed in humility. These are the ones who grow strong in the Lord. They are the greatest in the kingdom, and a pathway of death opens up before anyone who scandalizes them: it would be "better for [such a person] if a millstone were hung round his neck and he were cast into the sea" (Lk 17:2).

By pure grace, we all entered the faithful people of God through baptism. We were invited by faith and the inspiration of the Holy Spirit to live as children, walk in God's presence, and be blameless (see Gn 17:1). St. Paul says in the first reading (2 Tm 1:6–7) to rely on his strength and protection. But as bishops we were also set apart to serve that people. We were chosen to help our brothers so that we might all become a poor and humble people, taking refuge in the name of the Lord (see Zep 3:12). In living out the Lord's calling to lead, sanctify, and teach his people, we are asked never to cause scandal or break away from him, never to become rulers, strange lords or princes for that faithful people. Such conduct is denounced by the prophet: "Her officials within her are roaring lions; her judges are evening wolves that leave nothing till the morning. Her prophets are wanton, faithless men; her priests profane what is sacred, they do violence to the law" (Zep 3:3–5). As long as we remain among that faithful people who walk trustingly, abandoning themselves to God, we will not fall into these attitudes that cause scandal. We belong to the same people from which we were taken in order to be sent back to them.

Pastoral Gentleness

This conduct required of us entails the virtue of pastoral gentleness—not a mere mental attitude but a fruit of the Holy Spirit (see Gal 5:23). St. Paul recommended to Timothy that the pastor take no part in quarrels. He must be "kindly to everyone, an apt teacher, forbearing, correcting his opponents with gentleness" (2 Tm 2:24–25). Pastors who love their people, as good Christians, always display a serene gentleness in their constancy and strength: St. Paul advised his disciples "to speak evil of no one, to avoid quarreling, to be gentle, and to show perfect courtesy toward all men" (Ti 3:2), and to "let all men know your forbearance" (Phil 4:5).

St. Ignatius of Antioch tells Trallia's faithful that "meekness is a force" and proposes it to himself as a weapon to fight the devil: "Therefore I need to acquire a great meekness, for it shall undo the prince of this world" (*Letter to the Trallians*, chap. 7:1–8). This shepherd knew that self-sufficiency and an ill-tempered, imposing manner had scandalized and scattered the flock God had entrusted to him, shocking it and abandoning it to the clutches of the wolf.

On the occasion of this 100th Assembly of Bishops, we do well to ask the Lord to strengthen us, to grow in our service to

God's people, with a gentle heart and the faith that can uproot the sycamine tree (see Lk 17:1–6). Let us ask for that meekness that is not aggressive, does not despise any of the little ones of the kingdom—a meekness that, as the offspring of charity, is "patient and kind, not jealous or boastful, not arrogant or rude, does not insist on its own way, not irritable or resentful, does not rejoice at wrong, but rejoices in the right, bears all things, believes all things, hopes all things, endures all things" (1 Cor 13:4–7). Ask for the meekness of Mary at the foot of the Cross, the gentleness of Jesus' eyes when he looked at Peter on that Thursday evening (see Lk 22:61) or invited Thomas to place his hand near his heart (see Jn 20:27). It is there, in that heart, that we find the source of pastoral gentleness (see Mt 11:29).

Mary, Always Present

ↄ⟋⟍

Homily at the Opening Mass of the 102nd Episcopal Assembly

PILAR, MAY 9, 2011

Mary is the woman who "is present," as the Church presents her to us today. She is beside the Cross of Jesus (Jn 19:25). She is in the midst of the disciples in the upper room (Acts 1:14). She was present throughout the entire life of Jesus, and now she is here at the very establishment of the Church. The disciples come to the upper room with her and are intimately united, engaged in prayer, awaiting the promise of the Father, just as Jesus had told them: ". . . for John baptized with water, but before many days you shall be baptized with the Holy Spirit" (Acts 1:4–5). This was the promise that would bring them to maturity and bestow the strength to be witnesses "in Jerusalem and in all Judea and Samaria and to the ends of the earth" (Acts 1:8). It was the promise of the Paraclete who would always be with them (see Jn 14:16), "the Spirit of truth, whom the world cannot receive" (Jn 14:17), "the Counselor, [who] will teach you all things . . . and bring to your remembrance all that I have said to you" (Jn 14:26).

While the first Christian community recalled and anticipated the fulfillment of this promise, comforting one another by their common faith (see Rom 1:12), Mary could not help recalling another promise made to her decades earlier: "The

Holy Spirit will come upon you and the power of the Most High will overshadow you" (Lk 1:35), and that memory strengthened the hope that the Holy Spirit would do with the early Church as he had done with her, overshadowing it so that Christ might be born in every man and woman who would say *yes* to the Lord's promise.

There is a mysterious connection between Mary, the Church, and every faithful soul. Mary and the Church are both Mothers, both virgins who conceived by the Holy Spirit, giving birth to the Father's sinless offspring. And this is true of every faithful soul. What the Wisdom of God says universally about the Church, she says in a special way of the Virgin, and individually of each faithful soul. (see Isaac Monastery Stella, *Sermon* 51, *PL* 194, 1865).

The woman "who is present" points the way to the Church and to every soul, so that they may also be "present," expectant, open to the Holy Spirit who defends, teaches, reminds, and consoles. That Spirit manifests the consolation awaited by Israel, which Simeon and Anna craved in their hearts, which led them to encounter Jesus and their own recognition (see Lk 1:25–26) of him as their salvation, light, and glory.

Spiritual Consolation

The Spirit, the foretaste of our inheritance (see Eph 1:14), marks us with a seal (see Eph 1:13) and anoints us (see 2 Cor 1:21–22). The seal and the anointing of the Spirit encourage and give shape to a comforted Church, a consoled soul. But we are not always mindful that living in deep spiritual consolation ought to be our habitual state. Even in times of tribulation, the person sealed and anointed by the Spirit should never lack peace of heart, which is the "first degree of consolation." The martyrs bear witness to this, and Jesus himself referred to it as well: "Blessed are you when men revile you and persecute you and utter all kinds of evil against you falsely on my account" (Mt 5:11). Mary, sealed and anointed by the Holy Spirit, overflows with consolation and praises the Lord God, seeking him throughout history (cf. Lk 1:46–55) and, in her sorrowful silence at the foot of the Cross, the grief-stricken inner peace of her patience, she continually recalls God's deeds throughout that history, for this is the foundation of hope.

I wonder if we, as pastors, are used to leading the people of God from a place of spiritual consolation, even when we ourselves are perplexed or grieved by afflictions or sufferings (see 2 Cor 1:3–5). Do we, like Mary, open our hearts to the Spirit, the Paraclete, who is the fountain of consolation? If we are troubled, the people of Israel and our hearts shudder "as the trees of the forest shake before the wind" (Is 7:2). Do we dare to open ourselves to the consolation promised by the Lord: "Take heed, be quiet, do not fear, and do not let your heart be faint" (Is 7:4)? What strength comes to God's faithful people when they sense that their pastors are guiding them from a place of spiritual consolation! That is the spirit that Mary set in the midst of the disciples, preparing them for the coming of the Holy Spirit.

Mary, "the woman who is present," is the primordial figure of both the Church and the faithful soul, the one who conceives Christ by the power of the Spirit, the woman of peace in the midst of sorrow and tribulation. The woman who was "raised to the glory of heaven, accompanies the pilgrim Church with maternal love, and with goodness protects her footsteps towards the heavenly homeland, until the glorious day of the Lord" (Preface of the Mass of Mary, Mother of the Church). That is how she is in Luján, silent, transmitting peace and comfort. That is how she lived and how she is loved by our faithful people, who, gazing at her, cry out from gladdened hearts. People who let the Spirit mark out for them the path to Christ—a simple people, poor and humble, who put their hope in the Lord, who want their children baptized at the feet of the mother. Unappreciated by the "enlightened" elites, alienated by the atheist left, and dismissed as superstitious by the unbelieving right—for her, they are sinners yet faithful children, able to let the Holy Spirit teach them and recall to them the way of Jesus.

And that is how we bishops want to see her on her feast day: a mother who is present with them and for them. May we, in the midst of her faithful people, ask her for the grace to live in spiritual consolation, even in the midst of tribulations, and from deep within that spiritual consolation, lead the holy, faithful people of God.

The Word in History

~~~~

Homily at the Opening Mass of the 103rd Episcopal Assembly
PILAR, NOVEMBER 7, 2011

Today's liturgy has a strong temporal accent: the established time, the fullness of time, three days, the hour. It brings us from God's eternal time to the smallest instant of human time. It is God's way, or, with a little elevated language, the "eternal-temporal divine" that, throughout our history, embodies Catholic understanding of the "eternal-temporal": "*non coerceri a maximo contineri tamen a minimo divinum est*" (see *S.Th.* III, q.1, art.1, obj.4). The readings we have heard form a summary of salvation history, from greatest to smallest, revealing the wonders of redemption. The eternal Son is sent, born of a woman, but in the little town of Bethlehem (see Mi 5:2). It was the fullness of time, but contained in that specific moment; those jars used for the purification rituals are transformed to contain the new wine. It was at once a literal reality and the promise of another wine—gallons and gallons of water that, as the poet says, blush with shame on beholding the face of God.

At the same time, everything is concrete: from the Word, eternal like the Father, conceived in the womb of a virgin, until the wedding feast, the scene of Jesus' first sign: changing water into wine. There is no room for any "heroic" gnosticism or Pelagianism. All is grace, tangible grace, poured forth out of love.

131

Everything is concrete: a mother and the eternal Son, born of a woman, along with friends and disciples. The mother speaks, intercedes, and finally gives the order, but always with reference to her Son: "Do whatever he tells you" (Jn 2:5). She leaves room for the eternal Word to pronounce the word of the moment, there at Cana. And that Word in which all things were created (see Col 1:16), in which everything exists (see Col 1:17), takes the six stone jars in hand and makes the servants collaborators in salvation. The large and the small, side by side, and a mother's mediation, making possible the dialogue between the eternal and the temporal, so that God might continue to involve himself in our journey.

The Mediation of Mary

To place himself humanly within our history, God had need of a mother, and so he requested one from us. This is the mother to whom we look today: the daughter of our people, the servant, the pure one, God's only one, the discrete woman who makes room for her Son to perform the sign: the one who is always making this reality possible—not as superior or even protagonist, but rather as a servant, the star who knows when to dim and let the sun shine through. That is the mediation of Mary, which we observe today. It's the mediation of a woman who, far from renouncing her motherhood, takes it on from the beginning, with a twofold birth: first in Bethlehem and then again at Calvary. It is this motherhood that also embraces and accompanies the friends of her Son, her single point of reference until the end of time.

And so Mary remains with us, "placed at the very center of that enmity, that struggle which accompanies the history of humanity" (*Redemptoris Mater,* 11). She is a Mother who opens channels so that grace may flow freely—a grace that revolution-izes and transforms our lives and our very identity. The Holy Spirit, who makes us adopted sons and daughters, frees us from all slavery and, in a real and mystical possession, gives us the gift of freedom and cries out from within us the invocation of our new birthright: Father!

Today we venerate her as Mother and handmaid, the one who precedes Christ on the horizon of salvation history (see *Redemptoris Mater*, 3), who accompanies the Church, strength-ened by Christ's presence, walking in time towards the end of all ages, towards the encounter with the Lord. In this way, the Church follows in the footsteps of the Virgin Mary, who advanced on her pilgrimage of faith, loyally maintaining that union with her Son all the way to the Cross (*Redemptoris Mater*, 2). We ask her, as a good Mother who knows how to set things in order, to make room in our hearts so that, in the midst of the abundance of sin, the grace of the Spirit that makes us free chil-dren may abound as well.

In reflection and contemplation of these heartening and consoling realities on this first day of the month dedicated to her, the Cause of our Joy, let us allow ourselves, with the bold-ness and familiarity of true children, to salute her with the words of Scripture: "O daughter, you are blessed by the Most High God above all women on earth; and blessed be the Lord God, who created the heavens and the earth, who has guided you to strike the head of the leader of our enemies. Your hope will never depart from the hearts of men, as they remember the power of God. May God grant this to be a perpetual honor to you, and may he visit you with blessings, because you did not spare your own life when our nation was brought low, but have avenged our ruin, walking in the straight path before our God" (Jdt 13:18–20).

On the Social Doctrine
of the Church

&

Building a Culture of Encounter

ꝏ

Transcription of the Speech at the 12th
Day of Social Pastoral Care

BUENOS AIRES, SEPTEMBER 19, 2009

I once heard Cardinal Quarracino say that Argentina has been called "the country of missed opportunities." That comment has stuck with me. Sociologists and political scientists will tell us whether it's true or not, but it caused me to ask: *Is* Argentina a country of missed chances? If there were a Nobel Prize for failure to take advantage of opportunities, would Argentina win it? I do not know the answer to that question, and it leads me to the conviction of the urgent need to build and establish *a culture of encounter*; it urges the recovery and liberation from the current "autism" that shuts down historical memory, this community's engagement and capacity, decommissioning utopias of the future. These types of autism imprison us and lead to missed encounters. Is Argentina the land of missed encounters?

I like to distinguish between *country, nation,* and *homeland.* Simply put, the *country* is the geography, the *nation* is the entire legal institution (i.e., everything that gives legal and constitutional force), and the *homeland* is the living inheritance from our parents. I would say that we are not asked to be "regionalists" or "nationalists" but "patriots." The country, like many countries in other continents, if it suffers loss in a war, can be rebuilt. A nation that goes through institutional crises can rebuild itself, too, but if you lose your homeland, it is very difficult to recover it. The patriotic compromise that requires us to recover the outward culture of encounter aims to preserve the heritage of the homeland.

Allow me to read a poem from an author in the northern part of the country, written some thirty years ago. It's called "Our Homeland Died."

> Our homeland had died long ago,
> In the little village,
> It was not even an adolescent country.
> Just a child.
>
> Only a few mourned her: a little band
> Of schoolchildren.
> For most people
> It was an ordinary day.
>
> Over the white overcoat we placed
> The blackened braids,
> The Virgin of Luján and a round
> And blue rosette.
>
> Some very wise men told us,
> "It was better that she die."
> "It was just a country," said
> The people of the village.
>
> Yet we were sad. That homeland
> Was our homeland,
> It is very sad to be a homeland orphan.
> Later on, we understood.

It *is* very sad to be a "homeland orphan." The process of becoming one is not immediate; it takes decades, and it undermines the capacity for an encounter; it slowly encapsulates us in our status as orphans. Gradually we lose the reference points given us by our parents to make it grow and send it forward into new ideals.

Encounter through Dialogue

Perhaps the most suitable instrument for recovering a culture of encounter is awakening the capacity for dialogue. When one recovers the outward focus of the encounter, one begins to dialogue, and this means not only *hearing* but recovering the ability to *listen*. The other person, even if ideologically, politically, or socially on the opposing side, always has something good to give me, and I always have something good to give him. At that encounter, from which I draw good things, we can build a creative and fruitful synthesis. The dialogue is fundamentally fruitful; monologues lose their way. One of Argentina's great thinkers, Santiago Kovadloff, recently spoke of the danger of homogenizing the word, but even worse—the worst illness of all—homogenizing thought.

There is an "autism of sentiment" that leads us to conceive things in a bubble. For this reason we must recover otherness and dialogue. The dialogue is the ideal instrument for breaking away from all that burdens us, breaking out of closed ideologies and opening horizons through the little bit of transcendence that listening to each other entails. To dialogue is to transcend the situation in history, to lay a foundation of history for the future, to be able to leave an inheritance. To dialogue, ultimately, is to imitate God, who opened his dialogue with us by showing us the path to living together in fellowship.

In dialogue we recover the memory of the legacy we have received from our fathers, but not just to keep it "in storage." We receive a legacy so that it may grow within us, but we recover the memory. Through dialogue, we engage today's challenges together, making sure that the memory is embodied in the realities and responds to every present challenge. Through dialogue, we are encouraged, because it's not just "me" speaking, but many of us. Thus we find the courage to share our inheritance, and we fulfill our duty to make it grow, both for the present as well as for our commitment to future ideals.

A country of missed opportunities? I do not know. A culture of encounter? This is urgently needed, through the instrument of dialogue, because it is very sad to be homeland orphans. Let's not lose it, mistreat it, or throw it away. Let's not waste our inheritance or bury it. Let's make it grow. This is our homeland. If we lose that, we will be very sad, and we will have realized it too late. Keep working for this!

Social Debt and Human Dignity

⟡

Inaugural Conference at the Seminar on "Social Debts"

BUENOS AIRES, SEPTEMBER 30, 2009

During this presentation I will seek to give an overview of Church doctrine on the concept of "social debt." The Argentinean bishops in November 2008 affirmed that *social debt* is the great debt of the Argentinian people. This debt challenges us, and its repayment allows no delay.[1] Hence there is a need to cultivate an *awareness* of the debt we owe to the society in which we operate. And therefore we consider ourselves responsible for insisting on the social doctrine of the Church on the subject of social debt.

Social debt is not simply an economic or statistical problem. It is primarily a moral issue that affects us in our most essential dignity.[2] "[It] consists of deprivations which put at grave risk the sustainability of life, the dignity of man, and the opportunities for human flourishing."[3]

---

1. See *Hacia un bicentenario en justicia y solidaridad (2010-2016)* 5. Document of the Bishops at the closing of the 96th Plenary Assembly of the Argentinean Bishops' Conference, Pilar, November 14, 2008.
2. Ibid.
3. See *Para profundizar la pastoral social* 4. Letter of the Bishops in the Framework of the 88th Plenary Assembly, San Miguel, November 11, 2004.

An Existential Crisis

Social debt is also an existential debt crisis about the meaning of life. The creation of a full meaning of life goes hand in hand with the individual's sense of belonging to the activities of his daily life and the social groups in which he participates. Hence, the origin of existential emptiness refers, as Durkheim himself has said,[4] to a separation of the individual from the social environment—i.e., a lack of sense of belonging, which disfigures the identity. "To have an identity" involves primarily "belonging." Therefore, to overcome this social debt it is necessary to rebuild the social fabric and social ties.

The barometer of the UCA defines *social debt* as an accumulation of hardships and privations in different dimensions that make up the needs of the personal and social being. In other words, it is a violation of the right to develop a full, active, and dignified life in a context of freedom, equal opportunity, and social progress.

The ethical foundation from which to judge social debt as immoral, unjust, and illegitimate lies in the recognition of the serious damage that its consequences do to life, the value of life, and therefore human dignity.

"The greatest immorality," the Argentinean bishops say, "lies in the fact that it takes place in a nation that enjoys the objective

---

4. "[When the individual] individualizes himself beyond a certain point, if one separates oneself too radically from other beings, men or things, one finds oneself incommunicado with the very sources from which one should normally feed oneself, and one does not have anything to which one can apply oneself. In making a vacuum around oneself, one has made a vacuum within oneself and there is nothing left to reflect upon except one's own misery. Now one does not have any other object of meditation than the nothingness that is within one and the sadness that is its consequence." [4] A life without meaning implies a life without social rootedness. Emil Durkheim, *El Suicidio* (Buenos Aires: Shapire Editor, 1971), p 225.

conditions necessary to avoid or correct such damage, but unfortunately seems to opt to further exacerbate inequalities."[5]

This social debt is established between those who have the moral or political responsibility to safeguard and promote the dignity and rights of the people and those sectors of society that see their rights violated.

Human rights, as the *Santo Domingo Document* states, "are violated not only by terrorism, repression, and murders, but also by the existence of extreme poverty and unjust economic structures that cause great inequalities."[6]

Social Debt–An Anthropological Issue

The fundamental principle that the Social Doctrine of the Church (SDC) offers us in order to recognize this social debt is the inviolable dignity and rights of the person: a dignity that we all share and recognize in the less privileged and the excluded.[7] From this principle derives another one which guides human activity: As Paul VI and John Paul II tell us, man is the *subject, beginning, and end* of all political, economic, and social activity—each man, all of man, and all men.[8]

Therefore, we cannot truly respond to the challenge of eradicating poverty and exclusion if the poor remain *objects* targeted by the paternalistic and interventionist action of the state and other organizations, instead of *subjects*, where state and society

5. See *Para profundizar la pastoral social* 4.

6. Fourth General Conference of the Latin American Bishops, *Documento de Santo Domingo* (*DSD*), October 12–28, 1992, 167.

7. See Pontifical Council "Justice and Peace," *Compendium of the Social Doctrine of the Church* (*CSDC*), 2005, 153.

8. His Holiness John XXIII: Mater et Magistra (MM). Encyclical on recent developments of the social question in the light of Christian doctrine, May 14, 1961, 219.

generate the social conditions that promote and safeguard their rights and enable them to be builders of their own destiny.

In the encyclical *Centesimus Annus*, Bl. John Paul II warned of the need to "abandon a mentality in which the underprivileged—people and nations—are considered a burden, or annoying inconveniences eager to consume what others have produced." "The poor," he writes, "demand the right to share in the joy of material goods and to make fruitful their capacity for work, thus creating a more just and prosperous world for all."[9] Along these lines, we must affirm today that the *social* question—social debt—at its root becomes an *anthropological* question.[10]

Far beyond the logic of commerce, with its parameters and the rules within which the market functions, there is something due to man because he is man, by reason of his lofty dignity. This something due is inseparable from the opportunity to survive and participate actively in the common good of humanity.[11] In this sense, "it is a duty of justice and truth to not leave unsatisfied basic human needs so that those burdened by them may not perish. It is also necessary to help these needy people acquire the knowledge to enter the relationship circle, and to better develop their skills and resources."[12]

Causes of Social Exclusion

Social exclusion affects the very origins of belonging to the society in which we live, for the excluded find themselves not merely

---

9. His Holiness John Paul II: *Centesimus Annus* (*CA*), Encyclical on the Centennial of *Rerum Novarum*. May 1, 1991, 28.

10. His Holiness Benedict XVI, *Caritas in Veritate* (*CV*), Encyclical on integral human development in charity and in the truth, June 29, 2009, 75.

11. His Holiness John Paul II: *Centesimus Annus* (*CA*) Encyclical on the Centennial of *Rerum Novarum*, May 1, 1991, 34.

12. Ibid.

at the bottom, or on the outskirts, or powerless, but outside. The excluded—to whom we are in debt—are not only exploited, but are thought of as "surplus" and "disposable."[13] Today's culture[14] tends to propose lifestyles contrary to the nature and dignity of the human being. The main impact of the idols of power, wealth, and ephemeral pleasure has become, more than the value of the person, the high standard of performance and the decisive criteria in social organization.

The economic and social crisis, and the consequent increase in poverty, has its causes in policies inspired by those forms of neoliberalism that consider profits and the laws of the market as absolute parameters, to the detriment of the dignity of people and nations. In this context, we reiterate the conviction that the loss of the sense of justice and lack of respect for others have worsened and led to a situation of inequity.[15] The consequence of all this is the concentration of material, monetary, and information-based wealth in the hands of a few, which leads to increased inequality and exclusion.[16]

In analyzing the situation further, we discover that this poverty is not something random, but rather the product of economic situations and structures, social and political, although other causes of misery may be found as well.[17] This poverty, Bl. John Paul II has told us, finds its origin within our countries in mechanisms that, imbued with materialism and not an authentic

---

13. Fifth General Conference of the Bishops of Latin America and the Caribbean. *Concluding Document* (*DA*), Aparecida, May 13–31, 2007, 65.

14. Bl. Pope John Paul II, November 16, 1980.

15. *Navega mar Adentro* (*NMA*). Document of the Bishops at the end of the 85th Plenary Assembly of the Argentinean Bishops Conference, San Miguel, May 31, 2003, 34.

16. *DA*, 22.

17. Third General Conference of the Latin American Bishops. *Concluding Document* (*DP*), Puebla, 1979, 29.

humanism, produce, at an international level, a richer wealthy class at the expense of an increasingly poorer lower class.[18]

This reality demands personal conversion and profound changes to the structures that respond to the legitimate aspirations of the people towards true *social justice*.[19]

Social Debt and Social Justice

The Second Vatican Council stated: "Excessive economic and social differences between members of our society, in our people, are contrary to social justice, equity, the dignity of the human person and to social and international peace."[20] Since the first half of the twentieth century, the notion of social justice has been included within the Church's reflections on its social teaching. It affirms that social justice constitutes a true and proper development of general justice, closely linked to social issues, and that it concerns the social, political, economic, and, above all, the structural dimension of problems and corresponding solutions (see CSDC, 201). In *Deus Caritas Est*, Benedict XVI says, "justice is the aim and the intrinsic criterion of all politics."[21]

Social justice prohibits one class from excluding the others from economic benefits. It demands that the wealth, steadily increasing due to the social economic development, be distributed among each of the people and social classes, so that the common utility of all, so highly praised by Leo XIII, should be

---

18. His Holiness John Paul II, *Inaugural Address* (*DI*) at the Seminario Palafoxiano of Puebla de los Ángeles , Mexico. January 28, 1979, III 4.

19. *DP*, 29.

20. Second Vatican Council , Pastoral Constitution *Gaudium et Spes* (*GS*), On the Church in the Modern World, December 7, 1965, 29.

21. His Holiness Benedict XVI: *Deus caritas est* (*DCE*), Encyclical on Christian Love, December 25, 2005, 28.

protected—or, in other words, be preserved intact for *the common good of the whole society.*[22]

Social justice points to the common good that, at present, consists primarily in the defense of human rights. According to the CSDC (388–398), these rights constitute an objective norm, the foundation of the positive right and should be recognized, respected, and promoted by the authorities since they precede the state and are innate to the human person. And this, with reference to the problem of social debt, points to the community dimension: "The Christian vision of political society attaches the greatest importance to the value of the community, either as an organizational model of coexistence, or as a style of everyday life" (CSDC, 392).

Integral Development, Social Debt, and Political Activity

Poverty requires us to be conscious of its "*social and economic dimension.*"[23] It is, before all else, a human problem. It has first and last names, spirits and faces. To become accustomed to living with those who are rejected and deprived of social equity is a grave lack of morality that degrades the dignity of man and compromises social harmony and peace.[24]

There is an inverse relationship between human development and social debt. It is not a notion of development lim-

---

22. His Holiness Pius XI: *Quadragesimo anno* (*QA*), Encyclical on the restoration of the social order in perfect conformity with the law of the Gospel in commemoration of Leo XIII's encyclical *Rerum novarum* (*RN*), March 15, 1931, 57.

23. *Hacía un bicentenario en justicia y solidaridad* (2010-2016), 5. Bishops' document at the closing of the 96th Plenary Assembly of the Argentinean Bishops' Conference, Pilar, November 14, 2008.

24. *Afrontar con grandeza la situación actual,* 6b, The Bishops of Argentina, San Miguel, November 11, 2000.

ited to its economic aspects, but one of *integral* development, which implies the expansion of all the person's capacities. The less development, the more social debt. Therefore, development and equity should be faced together and not separately, and when the inequity becomes commonplace, the atmosphere of daily political life, then the struggle for equality of opportunity is not even addressed from the political sphere and levels off downwards towards a mere struggle for survival.

Economic activity cannot solve all social problems through the simple application of commercial logic. It has to be ordered to the attainment of the common good, which is the responsibility above all of the political community. Therefore, one should keep in mind that separating economic activity, which has the sole aim of producing riches, from political action, which would have the role of attaining justice through redistribution, is a cause of grave inequalities.

The Social Doctrine of the Church maintains that one can live authentically human relations of friendship and sociability, of solidarity and reciprocity, within economic activity and not only outside of or "after" it. The economic sector is not ethically neutral, nor is it inhuman or antisocial by nature. It is an activity of man and, precisely because it is human, it should be articulated and institutionalized ethically.[25]

In referring to the *use of capital*, Pope Paul VI invited people to evaluate seriously the danger that the transference of capital to foreign countries, for pure personal profit, could occasion for one's own country.[26] John Paul II pointed out

---

25. His Holiness Benedict XVI: *Caritas in veritate* (*CV*), Encyclical on integral human development in charity and truth, June 29, 2009, 36.

26. His Holiness Paul VI: *Populorum progressio* (*PP*), Encyclical on the development of peoples, March 26, 1967, 24.

that given certain economic conditions and the absolutely indispensable political stability, the decision to invest, that is, to offer a people the opportunity of giving value to their own work, is also determined by an attitude of wanting to help and trusting in Providence, which shows the human qualities of the one making the decision.

Pope Benedict XVI, in his social encyclical *Caritas in Veritate*, repeated that all of this maintains its validity in our day despite the fact that the capital market has been strongly liberalized and that the modern technological mentality might induce one to believe that investment is only a technical act and not a human or ethical one. One cannot deny that certain capital may do good when invested abroad rather than in one's own country. But the bonds of justice must also be considered: how this capital has been formed and the damage it might entail for those persons not employed in the places where it was generated.

One has to avoid letting the employment of financial resources be motivated by speculation, giving in to the temptation of seeking only immediate benefits, instead of the sustainability of the enterprise in the long run, its proper service to the real economy, and the promotion, in a suitable and opportune way, of economic initiatives also in countries in need of development.

Nevertheless, it is not licit to relocate solely to take advantage of particular favorable conditions, or worse yet, to exploit without providing to the local society a true contribution to the birth of a solid productive and social system, an indispensable element of stable development.[27] Capital also has a native country, we might say.

In this sense, the need of an active, transparent, effective, and efficient state that promotes public policies is a new option

---

27. Cf. CV, 40b.

for our poorest and most excluded brethren. To ratify and render effective the option of preferential love for the poor (*DA*, 396), which springs from our faith in Jesus Christ (see *DI*, 3; *DA*, 393–394), requires that we relieve urgent needs and *at the same time* collaborate with other organisms and institutions to organize structures that are more just. Equally, new structures are required that promote a true peaceful coexistence.[28]

Social Debt Demands Social Justice

Social debt demands the realization of social justice. Together, we have to appeal to all of the social agents, particularly the state, the political leaders, financial capital, the business leaders, agricultural and industrial, the unions, the churches, and other social organizations.

According to various sources, there are approximately 150 billion dollars belonging to Argentineans abroad, not counting what is in the country outside of the financial circuit. The media also informs us that approximately another two billion dollars leave the country each month. I ask you: What can we do so that these resources are put at the service of our country in order to help address social debt and generate conditions for an integral development for everyone?

In our case, "social debt" is the millions of Argentinean men and women, most of them children and young people, who are asking us for an *ethical, cultural response of solidarity*. This obliges us to work to change the structural causes as well as the personal or corporate attitudes that generate this situation, and through dialogue to reach the agreements that will permit us to transform this sad reality of social debt.

---

28. *Hacia un bicentenario* . . .

The Church, in recognizing and speaking of the subject, presents once more its love and preferential option for the poor and marginalized,[29] with whom Jesus especially identified himself (see Mt 25:40). It does this "in the light of the primacy of charity, attested to by Christian tradition, beginning with the pilgrim Church" (see Acts 4:32; 1 Cor 16:1; 2 Cor 8–9; Gal 2:10),[30] and in accordance with the prophetic tradition (see Is 1:11–18; Jer 7:4–7; Am 5:21–25).

It is essential for us to deal with the problem of social debt because human persons, and especially the poor, are precisely the path of the Church; this was the path of Jesus Christ.

---

29. His Holiness Benedict XVI: Fighting Poverty to Build Peace, Message for the celebration of the World Day of Peace, January 1, 2009.

30. Fighting Poverty to Build Peace.

Bringing the Nearness of Christ
to a Disillusioned World

ↁ

Homily at the Closing Mass of the National Congress
on the Social Doctrine of the Church

ROSARIO, MAY 8, 2011

The readings the Church gives us this Sunday, marked by the joy of Easter, proclaim the blunt reality of our Faith: Christ is alive; he became a man and gave his life for our salvation; by his wounds we are healed; he died, was buried, and rose again on the third day. In this Easter season, we conclude the National Congress on the Social Doctrine of the Church, which is neither a simple code of demands and behaviors nor a partisan position, but rather the consequence of the message of salvation in social life. It is a dialogue between the risen Christ and our world. We look to the Lord in the Gospel and wonder: What did Jesus expect of each person who came to meet him? Certainly, their faith—a faith that was able to confide and trust, to expect everything from him and to express itself in acts of charity.

What if we look at our world today and wonder what spiritual attitude has produced this civilization? Don't we hear the word "disillusionment" echoing above all the rest?[1] There is a

---

1. In the economic realm we may find a certain "resignation" to the seemingly inevitable consequences of a globalized economy to which there are no *alternatives*.

(continued)

dialogue between Christ the Savior, with his proposals of justice and love, and a disillusioned world.

Hope for Our Disillusioned World

There are various symptoms of disappointment and discouragement, but perhaps the clearest one is that of "custom-made magic," the magic of techniques that promise better and better things, the approval of an economy that offers almost unlimited opportunities in all aspects of life for those who manage to be included, the enchantment of minor religious proposals to suit every need.[2] Disillusionment has an eschatological dimension: it attacks indirectly, bracketing any definitive attitude and, instead, proposes those little charms that serve as "islands" or "truces" in the face of despair at the direction of the world in general. Hence, the only human attitude that can break free of these enchantments and disappointments is to set the last things

---

This economic idea influences policy, stripping participation in it of any ethical connotations: a fatalistic attitude about who will be included or excluded from the system takes over. In the Church the word "disappointment" also appears when talking for example of what was expected "from the council" or, in Latin America, "what was expected" of social change. The loss of the general meaning of life and the resignation to the current state of things result in disappointment—which, evangelically, is reminiscent of the disciples of Emmaus. What "we expected . . . but . . . it's been three days . . ." could well be the expression of the hearts of many who walk away from a devastated Church.

2. What we call the Western world, configured in dialogue with Christianity, spreads its own disappointment to the degree that the economy is globalized and consolidated. Ancient religions do not resist the advances of modernity: they withdraw into fundamentalism or the esoteric but lack a comprehensive response to the problems of humanity. It is here that the Church should not mistake her role. Although she has been able to respond with a certain gallantry to the beatings of modern and contemporary thought—approaching the poor without falling into Marxism, incorporating technology without falling into functionalism—she runs the risk of losing the sense of her own mission.

before us and to ask ourselves in hope: Are we going from good to better, or from bad to worse? Then, the question arises: Do we have a solution? Do we, as Christians, possess the words and deeds that mark the path of hope for our world? Or, like the disciples of Emmaus and those who remained in the upper room, are we the first to need help ourselves?

A good dose of humility is required to respond to these questions and then, with this humility, to return to the gospel with the thirst for new wine in a new wineskin. The disappointment of the modern world within the third of humanity that lives and dies in the most frightful misery is not only disappointment but *despair*—sometimes enraged, sometimes resigned. It reminds us of those two Gospel passages that speak of the directions in which a life may point: the disciples who were going down from Jerusalem to Emmaus, and the man assaulted by thieves who went down from Jerusalem to Jericho.[3]

The two situations are similar: first, the pain of the wounded man lying semiconscious with no possibility of escape, giving the impression that nothing effective can be done; second, the self-conscious and reason-filled disappointment of Cleophas. In both lies the same lack of hope. And that is precisely what moves the tender mercy of Jesus, who is on the road leading them, who lowers himself, becomes a companion full of tenderness, hidden in those *small gestures of nearness*, where the whole word is made flesh: flesh that approaches and embraces, hands that touch and bandage, that anoint with oil and clean the wounds with wine; flesh that approaches and accompanies, listening; hands that break bread.

The nearness of the risen Lord who walks—unknown— with the little ones of the town, who rouses in many hearts the

---

3. Cf. Lk 24:13–35 and Lk 10:29–37.

compassion of the Good Samaritan, is all that can ignite the fire of charity, to return to society with the enthusiasm of the disciples of Emmaus and go forth to proclaim the joy of the gospel. It is about the encounter with the living Christ, but we must rediscover his approach to heal the wounded, to destroy disillusionment and offer the joy of human dignity recovered. There we will find the answer to the question that we repeatedly ask ourselves: How can we make sure that human dignity, so often trampled upon, exploited, diminished, and enslaved, is protected?

Nearness Is Needed

The key word is "nearness," and this is a two-way street. The Lord, who approaches us when we are sad and carries us, is the same one who later, in Emmaus, makes as if to go further. How many times has he helped us, and our eyes have not recognized him because we would not take the time to invite him to stay with us and share our bread? And the promise to pay us back "what we have spent besides" applies only to those who have received and cared for their wounded. To the rest, he will say, "I do not know you," and the dreaded "Depart from me"—the definitive hardening of anti-nearness.

"Nearness," or intimacy, is the context needed for proclaiming the Word, justice, and love, so as to meet with a response of faith. Encounter, conversion, communion, and solidarity are categories that make that intimacy explicit, the specific evangelical criteria as opposed to the guidelines of a merely abstract or spiritual ethic. The "nearness" between the Father and the Son is so perfect that the Spirit proceeds from it.

It is the Spirit whom we ask to awaken in us that particular sensitivity which leads us to discover Jesus in the flesh of our poorer brethren—those who are neediest and most unfairly treated. Only when we approach and care for the suffering flesh of Christ can hope shine in our hearts—the hope that our disillusioned world asks of us as Christians.

We do not want to be that fearful Church, enclosed in the upper room; we want to be the Church of solidarity, the one that encourages people to go from Jerusalem to Jericho, urging her faithful to approach the poor, to heal and receive them. We do not want to be that disappointed Church that abandons the unity of the apostles and returns to Emmaus. We want to be the converted Church that, besides receiving and recognizing Jesus as our traveling companion, undertakes the return to the upper room, returns full of joy to Peter, accepts the integration of its own experience of nearness with the others, and so perseveres in communion.

We can say that the measure of hope is proportionate to the degree of proximity between us. In an open Argentina, in which people of so many races and creeds live in better community, the ground is well prepared to nourish this proximity in all its splendor and nobility.